PAN AM CAPTAIN
Aiming High

Captain Bill Travis

Copyright 2013 by Captain Bill Travis

All rights reserved. No part of this publication may be reproduced, stored in a retrieval system, or transmitted, in any form or by any means, electronic, mechanical, photocopying, recording, or otherwise, without the written prior permission of the author.

Published by Trabide Publications
Gilbert, AZ
Email: Trabide@PanAmCaptain.com

Library of Congress Control Number: 2013934338
ISBN 978-0-9890937-1-2 Hardcover book edition
ISBN 978-0-9890937-0-5 Softcover book edition
ISBN 978-0-9890937-2-9 Mobi eBook edition
ISBN 978-0-9890937-3-6 ePub eBook edition

Editors:
Dave Foxall
Connie Travis Salvato
Marissa Salvato
Michelle Lovi

Front Cover Design: macre8ive/LogoDesignGuru.com
Back Cover Design: Michelle Lovi, www.OdysseyBooks.com.au
Front Cover: Airplane Photo: Yanik Chauvin at BigStock.com

Back Cover Photo by Dee Travis

Published in the United States of America

Table of Contents

Book Reviews	v
Introduction	ix
Chapter 1 – First Flight as Captain	1
Chapter 2 – Visualization and Goal Setting	9
Chapter 3 – Farm to Nashville to Detroit	17
Chapter 4 – Using Visualization Consciously	27
Chapter 5 – School and Factory Jobs in Detroit	35
Chapter 6 – Travis Family Origins	47
Chapter 7 – The Army Years	53
Chapter 8 – Pursuing the Dream	73
Chapter 9 – The Zantop Air Transport Years	85
Chapter 10 – Pan Am Years, The Beginning	111
Chapter 11 – Pan Am First Class Service	123
Chapter 12 – Checked Out as a Pan Am First Officer	127
Chapter 13 – Flying into Vietnam	133
Chapter 14 – Awarded a Training Captain Position	141
Chapter 15 – Checked Out on the Boeing 747	147
Chapter 16 – Flying without Fear of Terrorism	153
Chapter 17 – That Can't Be My First Officer!	155
Chapter 18 – The Celebrity Passengers	165
Chapter 19 – Famous Pan Am Pilots	177
Chapter 20 – A310, First 2-Engine Atlantic Crossings	181
Chapter 21 – The Great Storm of 1987 in London	187

Chapter 22 – Unscheduled Landing at Islip, NY	195
Chapter 23 – Hong Kong Kai Tak Airport	207
Chapter 24 – My Airline Heroes	215
Chapter 25 – Problem Passengers	221
Chapter 26 – Lockerbie	229
Chapter 27 – Near Miss at 32,000 Feet over Ireland	231
Chapter 28 – Delta Airlines, A Turnkey Route Purchase	235
Chapter 29 – The Final Flight	241
Chapter 30 – The Music Scene	247
Epilogue	261
Acknowledgements	263
A Fit Sexy Body at Age 80	265

Book Reviews

"PAN AM CAPTAIN: AIMING HIGH is an adventure story wrapped inside a memoir. Here is a slice of aviation history viewed through the eyes of Pan Am captain Bill Travis. The author takes you on a personal journey, coming up the hard way, joining the great Pan Am at the peak of its glory days, living through the airline's slow descent to extinction, making the most of each new situation. Captain Travis is good company for this journey, not just for the plethora of anecdotes and personal history, but also for what you'll learn about the skills of visualization and goal setting. This is a great ride, informative and entertaining. You'll be glad you took the trip."
   Robert Gandt, Author of SKYGODS: The Fall of Pan Am

"Bill Travis brings life to the famous song 'Come Fly With Me' by taking the reader along on his many flights with Pan Am. His words beautifully encourage the reader to pursue their personal dream with visualization as a positive partner in that pursuit. You will "want more" from this talented writer who will motivate you to also aim high."
   Claire K. Connelly, Author

"Every air-mile of Captain Travis' book is a delight—it is a verbal 'Route 66' of memories, personalities, places, and the people we've known. It's not just a Pan Am story though—it is an airline story, a musician's story, an Everyman's tale of individual effort and perseverance ... truly an inspiration! Thank you!!"
   Paula Helfrich, Author
   FLYING – A NOVEL with Rebecca Sprecher

"I found the book both informative and inspirational, not to mention very well written. I particularly appreciate the underlying message that having a dream isn't enough, that it takes work and perseverance to achieve one's goals. I think your message is especially important in an era in which there seems to be a growing sense of entitlement. I also enjoyed your accounts of encounters with celebrities and your confrontations with troublesome passengers."
Geoffrey L. Gomes

"*Pan Am Captain, Aiming High* is a story told with love—love of family, love of fellow colleagues, love of careers pursued. Each chapter exudes Bill's care and concern for the many people in his life who assisted him along his career paths. It is evident on each page that Bill told his story in such an enthralling way because he was blessed throughout his life by the vast experiences his jobs afforded him.

He set out to do what he felt he had to do to be successful and attain his goals. No obstacle was going to be insurmountable no matter how long it took him to reach his goal. Bill Travis tells his life story in an enjoyable, warm style with page after page of interesting and often exciting moments. Through dedication to doing the best job possible, Bill describes the importance of seeing or visualizing whatever path he was to embark upon.

This story is solid in its story line and can be inspirational for anyone of any age, especially if pursuing a dream is a goal."
Susan Anderson, Teacher

"*Pan Am Captain Aiming High* is a very interesting read and held my attention throughout. I have a son whose goal in high school was to become an airline pilot. His aviation career path was similar to that of Bill Travis' and he achieved that goal and is presently a captain for a major U.S. airline. Having been a former private pilot myself, I had a good understanding of the aviation flight procedures for the various flights that Bill so aptly described. It was almost like *being along for the rides*. The methodology, which Bill emphasized ... of *visualizing* and persevering to achieve his career goals ... should be effective for just about any career goal that a person might strive for and, hopefully, this book will encourage and influence its readers in achieving their own goals."

Flora ("Flo") Davis

Introduction

The subconscious mind never rests—it is always working. This book is about how to make your subconscious mind work *for* you. If you can set a goal and then visualize yourself realizing that goal, your subconscious will work quietly in the background, even while you sleep, to guide you on the path to achievement. There are excellent books available that discuss the subconscious mind, the theory of visualization, and goal setting in great detail, and I recommend reading them. While those books will provide you with the theory, this book goes beyond theory and demonstrates visualization and goal setting techniques in action, with real-life examples.

You'll see how I used visualization and goal setting techniques to program my subconscious mind throughout my life, from my early years working in Detroit car factories after I had dropped out of high school, through the years when I was learning to fly as I pursued my dream of becoming a pilot, to my eventual rewarding career with Pan Am.

It was a difficult road, but I kept aiming high.-

You'll learn how I used positive thinking and visualization to pass my oral, written, and flight tests; how I used visualization to improve my flying skills; and how failure was never an option. You can apply these same techniques to achieve your goals, whatever they may be, but you must also believe in yourself. You must have, or develop, a good, positive self-image—and be willing to work hard.

As I tell you about the events that shaped my life—in order to help you learn to shape yours—I'll share some of my exciting experiences in the cockpit while flying for Zantop Air Transport and Pan Am. These are true stories. Some will be exciting, some harrowing, and some will be a little humorous. Within these stories you'll get an inside look into what goes on in the cockpit and the minds of the pilots as they deal with potentially life-threatening emergencies and problem passengers. You'll also see how pilots control their own emotions in order to keep their passengers calm during an emergency situation.

This is Captain Bill Travis welcoming you aboard. I can't say there won't be any turbulence along the way—but I can promise you an interesting flight.

Pan Am Captain Bill Travis; Photo by Dee Travis

Chapter 1 –
First Flight as Captain

It was 6:00 a.m. on September 12, 1984 when I arrived at the Pan Am Operations office in San Francisco. I was reporting to work for my first flight as a Pan Am captain. I had finally made it. All my life I had a vision of where I wanted to be, what I wanted to do, and now the last of my goals was being fulfilled. In one hour and thirty minutes I would be in the cockpit of an Airbus A300 announcing over the PA:

"Good morning, ladies and gentlemen, this is your captain speaking. My name is Bill Travis, and I would like to welcome you aboard your Pan Am flight to El Salvador, with intermediate stops in Los Angeles and Guatemala. Once we're airborne, I'll give you more information on our flight. In the meantime, our flight attendant team will be making sure that you are comfortable and safe. So, sit back, relax, and enjoy the flight."

Even now, just the memory of that moment feels good.

It had been a long journey for me—from the farm in Tennessee to Detroit, working in the factories, selling insurance, playing in jazz bands, the army days, and then learning to fly. Then it was seven years flying cargo planes for Zantop Air Transport: two as first officer and five as captain. Then on to Pan Am, spending two years as flight engineer, and thanks to the economy and Pan Am downsizing, 18 years as first officer. Now, finally, it was time for my long-awaited dream of my first flight as a Pan Am captain.

I passed the check ride, which was such an exciting event that my wife and I decided to take a photo with me in my new captain uniform. Unfortunately, the office had temporarily run out of captain wings and the new supply wouldn't arrive until the following week; but we decided to take the photo anyway because it was part of an ongoing project of photographing Pan Am pilots. Therefore, since Pan Am pilots and aviation aficionados reading this book will recognize that the wings in this photo are co-pilot wings, I feel the need to explain why I wasn't wearing my captain wings.

Naturally, I was hoping and praying for a smooth uneventful round trip; an easy series of hops from San Francisco to Los Angeles to Guatemala to El Salvador and back again, with a layover in Guatemala on the return journey. But fate couldn't resist having a little fun at my expense, and putting a wrinkle in things.

The flight to Los Angeles, the third busiest airport in the United States, was routine in that there were no problems to deal with, but far from routine in that the scenery was spectacular on that bright, sunny morning. There was hardly a cloud in the sky, except for a few fair-weather cumulus clouds, and the visibility was unlimited—a perfect day for flying.

As we reached our cruising altitude of 29,000 feet, we could almost see the full length of the California coastline. We looked down to the ground where we could clearly see parts of the San Andreas Fault line that extends from Point Delgada in the north, through San Francisco, and continues south to below Palm Springs. That's the fault line that causes many California earthquakes and has perpetuated the myth that half of California will break off into the ocean someday. According to the seismic experts, that won't happen.

We had just leveled off at our cruising altitude when, much to our surprise, Crista, the purser, a Mexico City native with long black hair, penetrating brown eyes, and a sincere smile, came into the cockpit. With her lilting Spanish accent, she asked, "You gentlemen would like to have a cup of hot coffee to keep you awake on this long 45-minute flight to Los Angeles, no?"

"Yes, thank you, Crista, that's very thoughtful of you."

That was a nice gesture because flight attendants don't have much time to perform their cabin duties on a 45-minute flight, so we didn't like to cause them extra work by asking to be served anything when a flight was that short.

The captain reports for the flight at Pan Am Operations where he checks the route, the planned altitude, and the weather. Then he'll go to the flight attendant briefing room. The primary purpose of that visit is to inform the purser of the time en route, the weather, and any known issues or delays. With that information, the cabin crew is "in the loop," and the purser can better plan the cabin service. At this briefing, by his demeanor, the captain also sets the tone for the flight. His demeanor will let the flight attendants know whether he's going to be a demanding "skygod," or a supportive team leader.

The captain needs to let the flight attendants know that if they have any problems, they should let him know so he can provide all the support they may require, and that he will communicate with them continually, keeping them informed of any aircraft or weather problems that may occur along the way. By communicating with the flight attendants in this manner, the captain is employing the team concept of leadership, and at the same time showing respect for his crew. When the captain treats the flight attendant crew with this type of respect, they will return the same respect.

Crista handed us the coffee and then took a moment to bask in the breathtaking beauty of the California coast. She then asked what we were seeing up ahead. I pointed out the spectacular Monterey Bay that extends from Santa Cruz in the north to the Monterey Peninsula in the south. She remarked that it was such a beautiful area, then smiled and thanked us for the short guided tour, and went back to care for her passengers.

Farther down the coast, near the Channel Islands, the course took a left turn to the east, passing near Santa Barbara and Santa Monica, then inland over the city of Los Angeles, and a few miles to the east, past the Los Angeles Airport. We were taken to the east of the airport in order to merge with the traffic that was arriving from the east. As the inbound traffic allowed, we were turned back to a westerly heading and given radar vectors to intercept the approach and landing system to land toward the west at Los Angeles.

After we had landed, taxied to the terminal, and the passengers had disembarked, I started thinking about our second destination. I had flown to Guatemala many times before in a 707 as first officer, so I knew that the instrument approach was tricky at La Aurora Airport because of the surrounding mountains. There is a real risk of coming in too steep and fast. If that happens, then by the time the wheels touch down, there may not be sufficient runway remaining to stop. And if it has been raining? Well, let's just say that arriving high and fast and forcing a landing on a slippery runway is a good way to spoil everyone's day. But after 25 years in the air, I wasn't about to let that bother me.

The take-off at Los Angeles, the flight to Guatemala, and the landing and subsequent take-off at Guatemala were smooth as silk. Score one for the new captain; we were off to a stupendous start. The next stop: El Salvador.

El Salvador Airport was not particularly challenging, but this was the 1980s and the country was in the middle of a civil war. When we touched down, we could see all kinds of military vehicles filled with soldiers, and several of these vehicles rode alongside us as we taxied to the terminal. But we continued to concentrate on the job at hand and just hoped they were there as an escort—for our protection.

The passengers disembarked, and then the crew had three hours to wait until the scheduled return flight to San Francisco.

Due to the war, it wasn't safe to leave the airport, but for our own security we weren't even allowed to get off the airplane. The crew rested up as best we could and tried not to think too much about the armed forces that might be planning to storm the country's only international airport. Still, we made it to the end of our break without incident, and pretty soon we were back in the air, returning to Guatemala where we could look forward to a 24-hour layover while another crew took the flight onward to San Francisco. So far, so good; my first trip out as captain was going well. There were no mechanical problems, no passenger problems, there was good weather, and my crew—highly experienced first officer, flight engineer and supportive flight attendants—had made the job easy for me. Everything was nice and uneventful, just the way every pilot likes it.

The next day, well-rested, we took off from Guatemala and headed north. The rest of the trip was in another Airbus A300, and it was now that fate chose to play a small but tricky card. Before we reached the Mexico-U.S. border, the oil gauge showed a leak in the number one engine. The A300 was a two-engine jet, and if one of the engines failed, FAA regulations dictated that we land at the nearest suitable airport, which at this point would have been in Mexico—not a big problem from a pure piloting perspective, but for a planeload of passengers expecting to land in Los Angeles, it would be a major inconvenience.

I won't pretend that oil leaks are everyday occurrences, but I will say that training always pays off. After sparing just a moment to think, "Damn, why did this have to happen on my first captain flight?" I got on with the job. The flight engineer began monitoring the gauge closely, to check just how fast the oil was leaking and whether we could make it to Los Angeles. I had the first officer contact Pan Am Operations in Los Angeles to advise them of our situation, so it wouldn't be a surprise to them if we had to land in Mexico; and if we did, then they could begin making plans to accommodate our passengers. The other big risk with an oil leak is a fire in the engine; so as one could imagine, we all kept very alert to that possibility.

I asked Crista to come to the cockpit and I explained the situation to her, so she could then keep the cabin crew in the loop. Until we needed to take a course of action, however, it was not necessary, nor desirable, to notify the passengers. After all, it would only cause unnecessary stress, maybe even panic, and we wanted them to relax and enjoy the flight. It was our job to do the worrying. If we did have to land early, I would make an announcement and the flight attendants would take over from there to keep the passengers reassured.

Now it was time for me to begin planning for a possible one-engine landing; a situation so rare that during my 35-year airline pilot career, I only had three engine failures. Two of them were on the two-engine C-46 while I was with Zantop Air Transport, and the other one was in the four-engine Boeing 707 with Pan Am. Consequently, the only time we would normally experience a one-engine approach was during our proficiency check in the flight simulator every six months.

In order to prepare for the possible one-engine landing, I asked Jim, my first officer, to watch the airplane while I close my eyes for a few minutes. Mike, our flight engineer, then turned his seat to face forward so he could assist Jim in watching outside for traffic.

As I laid my head back against the headrest, I began to go through the entire engine-out procedure: from the time we would shut the engine down, to making the approach, then the landing and taxiing in on one engine. I visualized myself performing each procedure: shutting the engine down, adjusting the airspeed to compensate for the loss of thrust, adjusting the elevator to compensate for the loss of lift, adjusting the rudder control to compensate for the higher thrust on one side of the airplane, and then reading the "Engine-Failure Check List" to make certain all of the items had been performed.

Then I visualized myself flying the complete approach and making a smooth, safe landing. After going through this visualization process, the approach procedure was fresh in my mind and my subconscious mind was programmed with the goal of making a smooth, safe landing. My subconscious, having been programmed, would help guide me in following that same procedure if we actually had to make the one-engine approach. Then I opened my eyes and told Jim and Mike that I was back in the loop.

Mike calculated the amount of oil that was leaking, and told me that if the oil leak didn't get any worse we could make it to Los Angeles before running out of oil. We all mentally touched wood, rubbed a lucky rabbit's foot, crossed our fingers and flew on. Soon we passed the point where landing in Mexico would not be necessary. That was one big step closer to home, but we were far from being out of the woods because the next potential alternate airport was Lindbergh Field, in San Diego.

I did not want to land at Lindbergh Field!

Unlike many other metropolitan airports, at Lindbergh Field the city is built-up right to the end of the runway with high buildings on either side of the approach path. If a fire or sudden engine failure occurred on the final approach, things could become dangerous very quickly. Landing on one engine can be done safely, but those buildings posed a risk. I decided that if we had to land in San Diego, we would confer with Pan Am Operations about the possibility of heading for one of the nearby military bases instead of Lindbergh Field.

Any time there's a major decision like that, and plenty of time to make it, a responsible captain coordinates with Operations, who in turn can involve the Chief Pilot if necessary. I didn't intend to be irresponsible on my first time out as captain. Besides, better decisions are made when there are several experienced people involved in the decision-making process.

Fortunately, fate was only having a little fun with us that day. There was no fire, both engines kept running, and the oil lasted until we landed safely at Los Angeles. After arriving at the terminal, I stood at the cockpit door, relieved, smiling, and saying goodbye to our passengers who had enjoyed a safe and comfortable flight. Little did they know what sometimes happens behind the scenes on what appears to be the most routine of flights.

As for the leak, it turned out to be a faulty seal that was repaired within an hour; we then proceeded on home to San Francisco—on schedule. Whew! After this first trip as captain, I could feel some of the stress that builds up inside when dealing with a touch-and-go situation. It was time to go home, have a cold beer, and celebrate my first flight as a Pan Am captain with my wife, Dee, who was so instrumental in my being able to achieve this goal in the first place.

Chapter 2 – Visualization and Goal Setting

Success

Success can be measured differently by each individual. It may be the amount of money you earn, where you go on vacation, or the status of your job. Of course, success doesn't have to be measured in terms of finance or status; the most important measure may be just doing something that fulfills your life and makes you want to get up in the morning.

As a young adult, it seemed I was destined to spend my life working in the factories of Detroit, but I had a vision. I wanted a better life for myself, and was prepared to make one. The only problem was I didn't know how. But that didn't matter so much once I had the vision of that better life, because almost without realizing it, I had begun to set goals that would guide me toward achieving that vision. Of course, I also had to work really hard to achieve those goals, and it didn't hurt to have the understanding and support of my parents, and later, my wonderful wife, Dolores, whom I call "Dee". Thanks to that initial vision of a better life, I was eventually able to get out of the factories and become a successful Pan Am airline pilot.

Why a Book, Why Now?

I retired from flying in 1992, and for many years, my wife, family, and friends were telling me that I should write a book about my history with Pan Am. It sounded like a good idea, and I knew I would enjoy reliving and sharing some of my memories, but I just could not fathom why anyone would want to read a book about me. *How boring*, I would think. After all, flying might be a challenge, and it's certainly a fun and exciting occupation, but sitting in the cockpit for eight hours across the Atlantic or Pacific Ocean is extremely dull most of the time. There are, however, occasional moments when things go terribly wrong, and then it's a cocktail of adrenaline and sheer terror. But unless I wrote about scary near-disasters, or fabricated some sex stories, I didn't think the book would interest anybody.

The thought of writing a book, however, never completely went away; it hung around in the back of my mind for a long time. Let's face it, people kept suggesting it—how could I forget? I have to admit that I was interested in writing a book, and had already written a number of blogs about Pan Am, but in order to write a book I felt I needed something special to say that would be valuable to my readers.

In September 2012, I had one of those eureka moments. I woke up in the middle of the night, sat straight up in bed, and saw the proverbial light bulb burning in my brain. It was like a neon road sign flashing, "This is it!"

It suddenly came to me how I had traveled my winding road to success. It wasn't a fluke, it wasn't just chance—there had been a method all the time. I just hadn't been consciously aware of it. Then, I realized that the same thinking and process that guided me along my career path could also help—and maybe inspire—others to find their own way through the uncertain maze that we call life. The book didn't have to be just about Pan Am. It could show how I used visualization and goal setting to get out of the factories, get my education, and finally become an airline pilot—and how I continued to use visualization to improve my flying skills throughout my entire aviation career.

Switching on the Light

The initial power for that neon light came from taking part in an online discussion forum. A number of participants were discussing how many people in the Phoenix area have to work for minimum wage, which was $7.65 per hour at the time of the discussion. Some forum members said they felt that anyone on minimum wage should hold back on their effort and give less than 100% because they're being underpaid. This didn't sit too well with me. Maybe it's the strong work ethic I inherited from my parents, but I've always felt that if one accepts a job for a certain amount of pay, then the worker should give at least 100% of the agreed upon effort.

It seemed to me that in having accepted a job, to put in less effort than the job requires isn't fair to the employer, and it's certainly a sure way to stay in minimum wage jobs. When I thought about it, as a teenager and young man, I worked for the equivalent minimum wage, but I certainly didn't want to do that for the rest of my life. So, that got me to thinking about how I had climbed out of my situation, and I came to the conclusion that giving anything less than 100% effort wasn't the answer.

When that neon light ruined my night's sleep, it was telling me that I should write my book and the focus should be inspirational. I could tell people not just about my Pan Am flying career, with some of the interesting and exciting experiences, but also show them how they can use the same tools of positive thinking, visualization, and goal setting to achieve their success.

So, that's how I came to write the book you're reading now. I decided that I could tell the story of how I achieved my success, and the techniques I used. But it was a long journey. Success didn't happen overnight. It happened over many years with a lot of hard work.

Visualization and Goal Setting Techniques

The techniques that I want to discuss in this book are not for the express purpose of helping anyone get rich—although if that's your vision you can achieve it. This book is for those interested in learning how it is possible to overcome seemingly impossible odds and achieve success by using visualization and goal setting. The emphasis here is on practical, simple techniques that anyone can use. I'm not going to get technical or theoretical. This is about how I, as a layperson, used these techniques. I want to tell you the story of my journey through life—from Tennessee to Detroit to California, from the farm to the factories to flying airplanes—and to show how these techniques worked for me, without me even consciously knowing that I was using them. I want to show how the same techniques can work for you.

If the theory and the science of these techniques interest you, and if you want to delve further into visualization and goal setting, then I highly suggest that after reading my book, you also read some of the books written by professionals in those fields.

Dreams Are Not Enough

If you can dream it you can do it. But don't kid yourself that all you need to do is wish upon that star and then sit back, relax with a cold one, and just wait for success to come to you. You must be willing to put in the hard work to make the dream you envision become a reality. Most successful people did not achieve their success easily—it took hard work and dedication. Nevertheless, if you set clear goals—short, medium and long term—I promise that while you're putting in the hard work, your subconscious mind will also be guiding you on the path to achieve those goals.

This book is about achieving your dreams. It's about how, if you know how to set goals, you can achieve just about anything you desire.

Of course, I'm not going to pretend that there aren't limits to that statement; an individual's physical and mental capabilities do set some boundaries. For example, if you don't have the necessary cardiovascular system or muscular structure, and can't develop it, then you're probably not going to be a top marathon runner, boxer, or football player, no matter how hard you train. You won't be a major league pitcher if you don't possess the upper arm strength and coordination needed for the job. Likewise, almost anybody could study and put in the hours to become a top-notch physicist, but not everybody can be an Einstein no matter how hard they study.

Some dreams require a little inborn talent, but we can, however, achieve the dreams that are within our physical and mental capabilities. I should mention that, while it's rare, there are people who have overcome extreme physical and mental barriers to achieve goals that were thought to be next to impossible. So, if sports are your thing, don't be too quick to dismiss those major league ambitions.

Sports Was Not For Me

While I'm sharing with you how I ended up as an airline pilot, let me tell you why I didn't turn out to be a sports athlete. I learned—or should I say, decided—at a very early age that I was not cut out for sports.

At around age 10, my friends and I played tackle football. We had played touch football before, and that was no big problem for me—touch football was fun. But on this day, we decided to play tackle; after all, we were big boys now—it was time we played the grown-up game. But tackle didn't go so well for me. On one particular play, I had the ball and was running toward the goal line, thinking I was doing great—free and clear. I had that goal line in my sights, thinking I would be over it in just a couple more seconds, just a couple more steps, when all of a sudden someone grabbed me by the shirt collar from behind, yanked me backward and slammed me hard into the ground.

No touchdown for me on that play!

My body was thrown to the ground so hard my back and head ached for the rest of the day. I said to myself, *no more tackle football*. Looking back, I guess part of me decided that I obviously didn't have the physical capacity to take the type of punishment a football player must endure. So, being a football player was never a goal and wasn't programmed into my subconscious. In fact, what I did after that tackle was effectively program myself to NOT become a football player.

As for baseball, thanks to another unfortunate experience, that was a game I never even tried. One day, I was out riding my bike and up ahead of me was a group of boys playing baseball in the street. I'm pedaling along, thinking the pitcher was going to wait until I passed, but apparently, he hadn't even noticed me coming. Instead of waiting, the pitcher threw the ball and—just my sporting luck— the batter swung with everything he had and made a solid hit. It was probably the best hit of the game. I could hear the crack of the bat as it connected with the ball, sending a line drive straight at me. The ball smacked straight into my forehead and knocked me off my bike onto the hard paved road.

There was no malice; it was simply boyish carelessness. They either didn't see me, or just didn't think I would get hit. Of course, they came over and apologized, helped me stand up, and I went groggily on my way. But I had a knot on my head for a couple of weeks. A little like football, I probably didn't have the physical makeup for baseball anyway, but the idea of being smacked in the head with a baseball didn't appeal at all. That incident ruled baseball out as a career.

Chapter 3 –
Farm to Nashville to Detroit

I was born in 1933 in a small farmhouse in Shelter Branch, an area of just ten houses in Dickson County, Tennessee. The house was home to my father's parents, people who worked the land for their living. To them, being an airline pilot would have probably seemed a very strange and distant ambition. My mother's parents were also farmers, but unfortunately, my maternal grandmother was one of the approximately 675,000 Americans who died of influenza during the flu pandemic that lasted from 1918 to 1920. Soon afterwards, my mother had to quit school to help her father care for her younger siblings and work on their small farm. By 1932, her siblings were old enough to take care of themselves, and my mother could think about building a life of her own.

Leaving school early was common during that era, especially in agricultural areas. Like many boys, my father had to quit in the sixth grade to help his family work the farm. Farm life was not easy during that period; it was all work—and especially for teenagers—not much time for play. Farming tended to be a case of baseline subsistence, just struggling to grow enough for the family to eat. However, some farmers, such as my paternal grandfather, grew tobacco and cut and sold timber from their land as a source of additional income. Farm labor was supplied by the farmer and his family, plus a few migrant workers who would come through during harvest season. Another important source of labor was the neighboring farmers.

Each farmer would help his neighbor, who in turn would help him. Without this basic collaboration, it would have been extremely difficult for the farms to exist at all.

Because of the dependency on family labor, most farmers planned on their sons remaining with the farm and taking over when they passed on. However, in the twentieth century the world was changing, and many sons and daughters longed to leave the farm to go in search of a better life. That was the path my parents elected to follow.

Love at First Sight

Maybe it was a generational thing, but I've always had a strong sense of family and a deep interest in my own family history. As a grown man, I've done some research into my family tree, following the Travis name as far back as I can. When my parents retired and moved back to Tennessee, I would visit as often as possible and listen to the family stories and reminiscences. One day, my mother told me how she met my father.

The home where I was born—where my father's family lived—still stands today, and is only about a mile away from where my mother lived with her father and siblings. Nearby was a spring which provided clean, clear, delicious water, perfect for drinking straight from the ground. In my parents' day, this spring became a meeting place for some of the local farm kids in their late teens and early twenties.

One Saturday afternoon, my mother was at the meeting place with a couple of her girlfriends when my father came along on his horse, on his way to town for the evening. He stopped to have a drink of the spring water, which gave him the opportunity to talk to the girls. Apparently, it was love at first sight, because as my mother

Farm house where Bill was born. Photo by Bill Travis

told me, "He never got to town that night." Instead, they began their courtship, and I'm glad they did because they were wonderful people, and very loving, supporting parents. Had my father gone on to town that night, who knows whether they would have married? Maybe I wouldn't be here to tell this story.

Leaving Tennessee

In 1939, when I was about six years old, my parents made the decision to leave the farm and move to Nashville, Tennessee, to seek a better life. My first brother, Leroy, was born by this time, and my youngest brother, Bob, was born four years after we moved to Nashville. My father went to a trade school to learn to weld and then began working at a nearby factory as a maintenance welder. My mother went to work at another factory as a seamstress. History says that in 1939 we were nearing the end of the Great Depression, but at the time it was difficult to see that end coming. Industry was at least in better shape than farming, but the factory jobs that drew my parents to Nashville were far from stable employment. Consequently, Nashville would turn out to be a stepping stone for our family—not a final destination. Over the next few years, we moved to Detroit so my parents could work in the factories there, then back to Nashville, and finally back to Detroit for good.

For many years, I would go back to Tennessee during the summer to stay with my paternal grandparents on the farm for a few weeks, then to the home of my cousin, Clarence, for the rest of the summer. Clarence was my age, and my best friend. He was a rough and tough farm kid whom I respected for his ability to ride bucking calves, walk behind a mule handling a plow, and do all the other farm work that I wasn't strong enough to do.

Clarence had a lot of work to do around the farm, but there was always time for fun, and we had acres and acres of woodland in which to play. All the kids there went barefoot during the summer because shoes were expensive, and we wore them out very fast. Fortunately, it only took a couple of weeks of walking on those gravel roads to get our feet tough enough so we could run barefoot as good or better than with shoes.

When I first arrived at the farm each summer and took my shoes off, my feet were so tender it was like walking on broken glass; the rocks were excruciatingly painful. My cousins would laugh and call me tenderfoot. But after a couple of weeks, the soles of my feet would be like boot leather. Then, running over the rocks was like running on clouds; I felt like I could run faster than greased lightning and I didn't miss my shoes at all.

During those hot, and often humid, Tennessee summers, one of the few treats we had each Saturday was a four-mile walk to the country store to have an RC Cola and a Moon Pie (this combination was later to become known as a "working man's lunch"). That was the extent of our sweet treats for the week. Then we would walk the four miles back to the house. Many years later, when my daughters were young teens, I took them to see my old summer stomping grounds, and although the old country store was long since closed and boarded up, we still found a place where we could enjoy my favorite treat of an RC Cola with a Moon Pie.

Even at that early age, I think I had the travel bug. I recall one day talking to Clarence and telling him that I wanted to get on a freight train and go somewhere, anywhere, and do something interesting. I had no idea where that somewhere was, or what I would do when I got there, but my mind was set on some sort of traveling adventure. There were no railroad tracks near the farm, so I don't know why a freight train was conjured up in my mind's eye, but I could clearly see myself standing in the doorway of one of those box cars as it rolled down the tracks. Looking back, that was probably the first indication of the path I would take; I obviously wanted to see the world, and being an airline captain certainly let me do that.

A Foggy Day in Nashville

When I was about seven years old, my parents took me to the Nashville airport to see off a visitor. Although I don't have any recollection of who that person was, or where they were going, something I saw that day imprinted an image on my memory so strong that I can still recall that image some seventy years later. In 1940, Nashville airport consisted of a single small terminal. In front of the terminal there was a simple wire mesh fence where people could stand and watch airplanes take off and land. The runway was about one hundred yards from the fence, and like any small boy, I was clutching at that fence, watching the airplane take off.

It was a dreary, foggy day, and just a moment after the airplane had lifted off the ground and passed in front of us, it disappeared. I was in awe of what I had just seen. The magic of flight had been heightened by the plane vanishing into the thick fog. The people on that plane had left the rest of us behind and traveled into some strange, mysterious world of cloud and mist.

It was a very simple event, but it carried such mystique for me. Even today, over twenty years since I retired from flying, whenever I see an airliner passing overhead, the image of that airplane taking off at Nashville airport and disappearing into the fog comes back to me. Did that image have anything to do with my ending up as an airline pilot? The skeptic would say possibly, but because I know that our subconscious guides us, then I have to say probably, even almost certainly. For me, that foggy take-off at Nashville airport so many years ago was one of many events that guided me down the path toward becoming an airline pilot.

Visualization is one of our most powerful mental abilities, and that power of visualization can help us to succeed in almost all of our endeavors. Sometimes, that visualization process takes place without us even realizing what's happening, and some visual images can remain in the subconscious mind and affect us throughout our lives. Therefore, it's important to learn what visualization is and how to use it.

By the time my parents retired and moved back to Tennessee, I was flying for Pan Am and living in California, but whenever I could, I would go to Tennessee to visit them. One day, as I was leaving the Nashville Air Terminal on my way to the car lot to pick up a rental, I caught sight of a photo mounted on the wall. Even though I had only seen the building in the photo once, decades earlier, I instantly recognized it. It was a picture of the original Nashville Air Terminal, the place where I got the first tiny seed of an idea that I might want to be a pilot one day.

History Repeats Itself

In 1959, I got my first airline pilot job with Zantop Air Transport, an all-cargo airline that flew automobile parts from Detroit to various cities around the country. In 1962, after becoming a captain for Zantop, I was scheduled to take a flight to Nashville. My parents still lived in Detroit at the time, but my mother's brother and his wife had remained in Nashville. Uncle Jimmy was my mother's favorite brother, probably because he was the baby of her family, and after her mother's untimely death she had become the mother to all of her siblings. Jimmy's wife, Corrine, became my mother's best friend. Because of their close relationship, I was also very close to my aunt and uncle, and since I was going to be at the airport for about two hours, I called them to see if they could make it to the airport to visit for a while.

It was a foggy day, with visibility limited to about one mile, but they only lived 20 minutes away, so they made the drive over and we had a nice visit. I don't recall if the wire mesh fence was still there, but my aunt and uncle did stay to watch my airplane take off. A few weeks later, I spoke to Uncle Jimmy and he remarked how eerie it was to see my airplane disappear into the fog shortly after take-off. I thought about how ironic it was that the foggy conditions on my first flight out of Nashville as an airline pilot were the same as they were some twenty years earlier when I stood awestruck at that wire mesh fence. It had been the same scene all over again. Only this time I hadn't been watching the disappearing airplane, I had been flying it.

Little Kids Should Be Seen and Not Heard

Unfortunately, not all visualizations are positive. Some vivid experiences can lodge in the subconscious and go on to have adverse effects on a person for the rest of their life, if they dwell on it and allow it to affect them, as I did. One such example involves another aunt of mine, and what she said to my brother Leroy and me when I was around eight years old.

Aunt Sally was a wonderful, kind and generous lady, who would often take care of us when our mother was working. I remember her gray hair pulled back in a bun, her horn-rimmed glasses, and the loose print dresses she used to wear. But one thing that stands out in my memory of Aunt Sally was that she played the organ; not the electric kind, but the type where the organist used their feet to pump air into the chambers to get the sound. That organ fascinated me, and anytime we asked her to play for us she was happy to oblige. While I don't recall anything about the music she played, I do remember enjoying it, and in that sense, Aunt Sally was one of my earliest musical influences.

We were always treated well, but Aunt Sally had some strict ideas about child care, and she was not reluctant to take a switch to us if we misbehaved. In those days, that was acceptable disciplinary behavior and quite common. Did it hurt? Of course it did, but more often than not, the mere thought of being "whupped" (as we said it in the south) was more painful than the actual whipping.

One day, my parents, my brother Leroy, and I had dinner at Aunt Sally's house. Leroy and I tried to get involved in the conversation, but Aunt Sally kept telling us to "shush up." Finally, she said we should keep quiet because "little children should be seen and not heard." The image of her sitting at the table and saying those words is one that I've never forgotten, and probably never will because I believe I allowed them to have a very negative effect on me. I have a shyness that I've never completely gotten over, and don't think I ever will. My younger brother, on the other hand, was not affected by Aunt Sally's remark. He was always gregarious—never shy. I guess that goes to show that one person's memorable, life-changing event is another's forgotten moment.

For me, looking back on this episode further reinforces my belief in the power of visualization as both a positive and a negative influence on our subconscious mind. Of course, I also know that we can work to address the negative influences by thinking positively, and I have put a lot of work into getting over my shyness. I have made great improvements but the underlying shyness is still there.

Chapter 4 – Using Visualization Consciously

Later on in life, I read a lot of books on positive thinking and visualization, including *The Power of Positive Thinking* by Norman Vincent Peale and *Psycho-Cybernetics* by Maxwell Maltz. Out of all the books I read, these two books stand out in my mind as having the greatest influence on my thinking.

Maltz used the analogy of the brain as a cybernetic "servo-mechanism", which is designed to automatically find a path to the target with which it is programmed. He used different words, but I would compare the brain to a computer and use the phrase: "Garbage in—Garbage out." If you program your brain with negative thoughts by saying, "I can't do that," or if you constantly worry about something not going right, then you are programming your brain to help you fail. You will not be able to achieve a goal when you've programmed your brain for non-achievement. Conversely, if you program your brain with positive thoughts, such as:

"I can do this,"
"I can be successful,"
"I can stand up and give that public speech,"

then you will program your subconscious mind to guide you on the road to success.

There are probably very few people who haven't heard the

children's story, *The Little Engine That Could*, a classic tale that teaches children the power of positive thinking, optimism and hard work. As goes the version written by Arnold Munk, under the pen name of Watty Piper, the long train of freight cars needed an engine to take it over a very high hill. All of the larger engines said they couldn't do it because it was too much of a load or too steep a gradient. Finally, a small engine was asked, and that engine said, "I think I can." As the little engine with the long train of cars climbed the hill, going slower as the going got steeper, it kept saying, "I think I can, I think I can, I think I can." Then, as the little engine finally passed over the top of the grade and began descending on the other side, it said, "I thought I could, I thought I could."

The larger engines programmed failure into their brains and wouldn't even try. The smaller engine programmed success into its brain; it tried and succeeded. It kept up the mantra: "I think I can, I think I can, I think I can," and that helped the little train to keep working hard until it succeeded. It never once said, "I don't think I can."

As I look back over my life's path, I can see clearly that I did the same thing every step of the way. When I programmed myself for success, I succeeded; when I programmed for failure, I failed. The key point here is that you can do the same thing. You always have a choice of attitude and programming, and you should program your brain with positive thoughts. I did. And if I can do it, so can you.

Remember: If you take some time to grasp the basics of how visualization works, then you've taken the first step toward controlling your future. Apply the computer analogy, Garbage In—Garbage Out. Stop filling your brain with negative thoughts, because that is what will come out. Keep working on programming your brain with positive thoughts and goals, and the subconscious will begin to guide you to achieve your goals.

However, you must go further than just programming the subconscious mind with your goals. You must also visualize yourself having reached those goals. If your goal is to be a trial lawyer, then visualize yourself arguing, and winning, a difficult trial case. Those visualizations give the subconscious mind a target. It's like programming your GPS so the navigation system can guide you to your destination.

On the road to the major long term goal, there will be short term and medium term goals that you need to visualize and set. Using the goal to be a trial lawyer as an example, one of the goals may be getting the money or scholarships to help finance the education. Therefore, funding would be short and medium term goals. Some short term goals on that road could be passing the courses with a certain GPA. The medium term goal would be getting the undergraduate degree. Another medium term goal could be getting accepted into the desired law school. For each of these goals, you would be visualizing having already achieved the goal. Then your subconscious will guide you on that road. But remember, you will need to do the hard work necessary to achieve the goals. You won't get a high GPA by dreaming—you must study.

While you need to be thinking positive, you must also be aware of the negatives because they will be there and you'll have to deal with them. Since the negatives will raise their ugly heads, there will be setbacks and failures. When you experience a failure, you have to work your way through it, then forget it and concentrate on your goal. Do not look back. Learn from your failures, but do not dwell on them. They're merely bumps on the road to success. Your subconscious is still guiding you toward your destination. As you're being guided to your goal, you will also need to work hard to gain the skills required of your goals, and the harder you work to gain and improve those skills, the fewer setbacks and failures you should experience.

Most people learn better when they use more than one technique, such as hearing, seeing, and doing. In the case of visualization, it can also help to verbalize the goals, as a method of strengthening the message, and share those goals with someone close to you. Achieving your goals will take some effort, hard work, and time. Success does not come overnight. So, as Larry the Cable Guy might say, cut out the negative crap and "Git-R-Done."

Visualization in Action for the Pilot

I'm going to jump ahead a little here and give an example of how I regularly used visualization during my flying career. Every six months, airline pilots put their job on the line when they're given an oral exam and flight proficiency check. This is a serious event. If a pilot failed a check ride or oral exam, they would be taken off flight status and given a few days to study and repeat the failed portions. If they failed a second time, then they would have an interview with the chief pilot to determine if there are any underlying circumstances, such as personal issues, that may have caused the failure. If they fail a third test, they could be asked to resign.

Well, I had spent so much time and effort working to achieve my airline pilot goal, that I knew I never wanted to fail even the first test. So, I developed a system to make sure that I would always pass my oral exam and check ride. About sixty days prior to the test day I would begin studying. After the study period, which would refresh my memory on all the non-routine facts and procedures that a pilot needs to know but doesn't use every day, I would visualize myself in the small interview room with the check pilot asking me questions. In that visualization, I would provide one hundred percent correct answers. Then I would sit down and imagine I was in the cockpit. I would visualize every single switch and dial in the cockpit and explain its purpose and function and how it would be used in an emergency.

Next, I would visualize myself in the simulator cockpit going through a complete flight, from the pre-flight check to taxiing out, making the take-off, then back to making a landing and taxiing in. I would go through every potential emergency, such as loss of pressurization, engine failure on take-off, engine fire, double engine failure, and so on, picturing myself doing exactly the right thing in each scenario. By the time I had completed those visualizations, I was ready for the check ride.

I never failed a check ride, because my brain was not programmed to fail. Failure was not an option. My brain was programmed to pass. It was hard work, but it ensured that I would continue to be a pilot and airline captain.

Setting the First Goal

The first time I recall consciously setting a specific goal was as a young man living in Detroit. We lived in the inner city, in a row house. Most all the homes looked the same, sort of an Archie Bunker style with three rooms downstairs arranged in shotgun fashion where we had to go through the first two rooms to get to the kitchen, and three small bedrooms upstairs. At the time, I was working in a factory during the day and playing drums on the weekends. One day, I was playing a music gig for a party at a private residence. Residence? To me, that place was a mansion!

We had to travel out to the suburbs for the gig, and when we got there we found a large home with a magnificently manicured green lawn, beautiful flower garden, swimming pool, and a small guest house in the back. The band was set up on a large covered patio area. I was amazed at the size and beauty of this home. A home with its own private swimming pool? WOW! This farm boy had never seen anything like that. Our swimming pool was a deep hole in the meandering creek that ran through Shelter Branch. I had never imagined anything like having a pool in my own backyard—we didn't even have a yard. The front stairs to the first level of our house were right off the sidewalk, and the back stairs went right down into the alley.

Once I got over the initial amazement, I started thinking: *I would love to own a home like this someday*. But, given my station in life at the time, that was some dream, and I could easily have continued the thought by saying to myself, *but alas, I'll never be able to afford something like this*. I could have taken the attitude that the trains with the big engines took, and said, "I can't do that." However, since it was not in my nature to take such a defeatist attitude, I decided that someday I would own a home like this.

I've always been a pretty positive person, inclined to see the glass as half full rather than half empty, but I still look back and am kind of amazed at my own youthful confidence and positive self-image. At the time, around 1951-53, that "mansion" was probably worth about $60,000, and I was making 60 cents an hour working in the factories. I would have to save the wages from 100,000 hours' work to buy that place, and even then I wouldn't be able to afford to maintain it. It was doubtful that a few dollars for each gig I played on the weekends would make up the shortfall either. But the fact is, I did tell myself: *someday I will own a home like this*. I kept thinking about that house for a long time, which is probably why I can still picture it in my mind today.

Without realizing it, I set a long-term goal and put my subconscious mind to work, helping guide me in my decision-making to navigate the road to that goal. After a few years at Pan Am, I was able to achieve my dream of owning a home like that the one from the gig. In 1978, we purchased a beautiful home in Danville, CA, with a one-acre lot where we were able to have two horses for our family to enjoy—and a swimming pool—in our own backyard!

The Importance of Sharing Goals

One day, before we were married, Dee asked me what my plans were for the future, and I had to admit that I really didn't know what I was going to do. But I did plan to work in some white collar job where I could earn $10,000 per year. Remember that starting point of 60 cents per hour? That's some goal—but I was aiming high.

When Dee and I met, I had already left the factories and was working for the post office. After I had been in the factories for a while, I decided enough was enough. The factory jobs were not going to give me what I wanted out of life, so I decided I had to get out and find a white collar job, and coming from a factory production line, the post office was a step in the right direction. I also decided that I wanted to earn $10,000 per year. I don't know where that number came from, but I remember it clearly. Working for 40 hours per week, 48 weeks per year, the annual factory wage was around $1,150. So, that goal of making $10,000 per year was a huge goal—clearly a long-term goal. But if I had set my goal at just $2,000, still a big improvement over my factory wage, then that would be what my subconscious mind would be programmed for, and that's all I would achieve. By setting that large long-term goal, and then setting smaller incremental goals along the way, the chances of meeting the $10,000 goal were greatly improved. Of course, I didn't know this at the time; I was just working on a combination of instinct and common sense.

If you're aiming low, you'll achieve low goals. If you're aiming high, you'll achieve high goals. So you should be constantly aiming high.

Not long after that conversation with Dee, just to prove that life will always make ones journey interesting, I was drafted into the army while the Korean War was winding down. About a year later, we were married and living off-base near Fort Hood, Texas. But my goals still stood, and in hindsight I know that by saying them out loud and sharing them with Dee, I had made some sort of commitment both to her and to myself. Over time, I have come to understand how important it is to verbalize ones visualizations and goals to others, and how that verbalization reinforces the instructions to the subconscious mind.

But I don't want to get too far ahead of myself….

Chapter 5 –
School and Factory Jobs in Detroit

Once the family settled in Detroit, I lived there a long time, right up until a few years after I got my first airline job, and my parents retired and went back to Tennessee. However, spending the mid-1940s moving back and forth between Detroit and Tennessee presented me with a particular issue to deal with—language. As a kid still in school, I was back and forth from Detroit to Nashville for visits and relocations so much that I had to learn to switch accents. There was a very definite difference between the Detroit accent and the Nashville southern dialect, and I had to master them both as a means of self-protection. Until I did, I was called a "Yankee City Slicker" in Nashville and a "Hillbilly" in Detroit. Nobody likes to stand out at school, so eventually I got to where I could drop in and out of the two ways of talking fairly easily; then I didn't get teased so much.

During the time we were in Nashville and up until I was in high school my grades were all A's, probably because I was interested in school and was comfortable in the environment. When I was reading or studying, I could always imagine myself having an interesting and enjoyable future. Trouble was, at the time, I lacked the specific vision to know what that future would be. After I got into high school, I started to lose interest in my studies. Looking back now I see that it was largely due to moving back and forth between North and South. My roots were in the farming region, and I didn't feel like I belonged in this new urban environment. For instance, some of the kids I knew in school played tennis, but I couldn't relate to the sport because I had never been around it, so I never socialized with these kids outside of school.

One thing I did enjoy was music. I had learned to play drums in elementary school, so I joined the high school band in Detroit and got a lot of enjoyment from being in the concert and marching bands. But the drumming alone wasn't enough to forge that school-social link, and consequently I began hanging around with the wrong crowd—kids who had not done well in school and dropped out to work in the factories. That's when my grades began to suffer.

Don't get me wrong—except for not wanting to study, these were good kids, but the lure of a factory job and making some money was strong in those days. Finally, the glamour of a regular salary got to me too, and since my grades were suffering, I elected to quit school after completing the 10th grade with a very low GPA.

Prejudicial Programming

Prejudice on grounds of color can be a very strong program in the subconscious mind, but I do not believe it to be a natural program. It is placed there, often by elder family members, and reinforced by similar-minded peers and the media. However, I was lucky; my parents never taught me to be prejudiced, so, fortunately, I was "color blind". But many other kids at the time were not color blind; they had learned to be prejudiced.

Back when I was growing up in Nashville, there was a black neighborhood about a half-mile from my school. I had stopped at a drugstore on the way to school one day, where I met a black boy my age and we began talking. We became friends and I would go to his house and play. I didn't understand why my friend's mother was always nervous about me being there, but I finally learned that it was because she was worried my parents would be upset with her for allowing me to be at her house in the "colored" neighborhood.

One day, when I was walking home from the boy's house, several boys, older and bigger than me, pulled me off the sidewalk, roughed me up, and told me that if I didn't stop playing with that N.... kid, they would beat me to death. They were serious—and I was terrified. That was a very sad day because I realized I wasn't going to be able to play with my friend anymore.

Racial prejudice was a fact in America at that time (and still is now), but it's something I could never understand. On another occasion, around the same time, I was the only passenger on a bus going to downtown Nashville. At this point, Rosa Parks and the Freedom Riders were all in the future. The buses all had a clear line with a sign designating the back of the bus for colored people; the black passengers had to sit behind that line. On this particular journey, a black lady got on and sat in a seat just in front of the line—probably because it was closer to the rear exit door—and the bus driver yelled at her to get to the back of the bus. That really bothered me, so I got up and went back to sit in a seat immediately behind the line. The driver did not look pleased, but there was no rule that said I couldn't sit there, so he didn't say anything. The lady later looked at me and gave a sly smile, as if to say thank you.

Much the Same in Detroit

Despite talk of a North-South divide on civil rights issues, I found things little different in Detroit. At a school dance class, the teacher had instructed the boys to go across the dance floor to choose a girl to dance with. There was one black girl, Sandra Thomas, and

I noticed that all the other boys had avoided her. I was very shy and found it difficult to ask a girl to dance, but I had no issue with Sandra being black, so I went and asked her. She was a nice girl and fun to learn to dance with. When the class was over and everyone was leaving, Sandra's brother came by the class to meet her. As I was walking out of the room, she stopped me and introduced me to her brother, James. He was a very friendly kid, with a beaming smile, who loved to make people laugh, and he and I eventually became good friends. I learned that he was also someone who would look out for his friends. One time, when I had a paper route and was robbed by a couple of larger boys at night while doing the collections, he volunteered to go with me on my route for several nights until I could gather enough nerve to again go by myself. That was true friendship. Sadly, after high school, I lost touch with James and Sandra. These relationships proved to be valuable to me a few years later when, because of having some black kids as friends, understanding that they were just like me, and liking and trusting them, I was able to proudly *refuse to accept* a job that could have made me a lot of money.

The World of Work

Before quitting high school, I had worked several after-school jobs, including mowing lawns, having a paper route, and working in a dry cleaning shop. My parents had a very strong work ethic, and always gave a lot of effort to their jobs. Fortunately, that work ethic was passed along to me, and as a result, I always gave 110% to any job I took. My parents did not like the fact that I quit school to work in the factories; however, they were always supportive of whatever I did. That helped tremendously, because I knew that whatever type of work I did, they would be there for me, and not be critical. They wanted me to do well in life, but unfortunately, since they didn't have an education themselves, they couldn't help me with school.

Before giving up on education completely, I decided to go to a technical school and study welding because my dad was a welder, and I thought that might work for me. Nice idea, but it only took a few weeks for me to decide that I was not going to be a welder. I didn't like working, almost in the blind behind a dark welding shield, and I did not do a good job on the assigned projects. That was when I made the decision to quit school for good and go to work in the factories.

Working in the factories was hard. It was also very repetitious and boring—the same rote movements all day long. Nevertheless, in order to earn more money, I would sometimes work two factory jobs at the same time because they were close enough together that I could finish a day shift at one and then rush over to the other to work the afternoon shift. Of course, that cut into my social life, which as a teenager was pretty important, so keeping the two factory jobs at the same time didn't last too long.

Frequent job changes were common in Detroit at the time. A hallmark of the factories in the Motor City was that during a model change they would shut down production, and most everyone would be laid off at the same time. Many of the workers would then get a job at another factory that wasn't in a changeover phase, while others would sign up for unemployment and take it easy until they were called back to work. Altogether, I probably worked in six different factories. The first job was very easy, and the last was so difficult I had to quit after just two weeks.

Kaiser-Frazer

I loved the look of the Kaiser cars, and working to build them for my first job was a special pleasure. My role was placing the leather dash pad in place on the Manhattan four-door sedan, and gluing the ends so they stayed put for the rest of the production process. At this position on the assembly line, the body was already connected to the chassis, but the front quarter panels, doors, and windows were not installed yet, so one could stand right in front of the dash and reach over to install the pad. I would install and smooth out the pad, glue it at the edges, and then grab a new pad and as I moved on to the next car.

This assembly line moved rather slowly, and I was working on the dash pads with two other guys, Mike Adams and James Moore. I remember Mike always wore a baseball cap. Now this might be a common sight today, but back then it was pretty unusual. James and I guessed that he might be bald on top and wanted to cover it up (after all, he was nearly 30!), but we didn't say anything. Anyhow, the three of us got along well, and it didn't take us long to figure out that since the line moved so slowly we could have one of us doing the job of all three while the other two took a break.

So, I would work for 30 minutes while the other two took it easy, then James would swap with me and work for 30 minutes, then finally, Mike would take his turn for another 30 minutes. We each worked hard for that half-hour—after all, we had to keep up, and besides, we wanted to do a good job—and by doing so, we earned an hour's break. Mind you, while each of us was working, we could not get behind because that would affect the next process on the line, and we didn't want to hold up the next guys or they would become very angry. So we learned to work hard, fast, and accurately. The work was inspected at various locations before moving into the next phase, and if the work needed corrections, the inspectors would report this to the foreman. We made sure we did good work.

This cushy number only lasted until the next model change when everyone got their customary pink slips. Often, the pink slips would come just before Christmas, which meant less money for presents and for the family at Christmas. But it was a fact of life in the factories—something we learned to expect and live with. Once the assembly line was set up for the new model, they would recall the employees. If they really liked the job, then they would probably go back. However, sometimes necessity would have forced them to find a job at another factory and they may have preferred to stay at that new job.

Cadillac

My last factory job was a killer. It was around 1950-51, and the Cadillac plant was only a mile from our home, which should have been a big point in its favor. I worked on the assembly line, hanging the right front quarter panel on an endless procession of Series 62 sedans. This was a large panel, all metal—very heavy. In those days I only weighed 125 pounds soaking wet, and I had to lift this heavy quarter panel, which hung from a moving conveyer, place it on the car, and get the bolts in place.

I think I could have eventually built up the strength to do this job well, but there was one insurmountable problem. When I came into work each morning at seven o'clock for a nine-hour work day, the person on the last shift had gotten behind. It wasn't cool to get behind on the line because it affected everyone beyond that position. But because of the shift change, I never got to see the person who had fallen behind, and complaints to the foreman fell on deaf ears. Consequently, I had to work like hell to get caught up every morning. It would take me two hours—up until my first break—to get back on track. We would have a fifteen-minute break in the morning, a thirty-minute lunch, and a fifteen-minute break in the afternoon.

Here I was, working until my morning break to get caught up; then as I went on my break, the relief man, who knows all the jobs, but is not very proficient in any, and has no incentive to keep anyone on schedule, would get me behind again. Coming back from break was the same as coming to work in the morning. I'd spend the next two hours getting caught up again, and then it's time for lunch. Got the picture? You know what then happened after lunch, and then after the afternoon break, right? Right!

Each night, I was so exhausted that I would go straight home, have a quick dinner, and go right to bed. I was a 17 or 18-year-old kid who was supposed to have endless energy. Well, I had the energy, but the job sapped it all during the day; it became so physically exhausting for me that I finally had to ask the foreman to place me on another job—one that I could handle. He refused, so I had to exercise my only other option.

I quit!

That was a solid turning point for me because the Cadillac factory job convinced me that I had to somehow get out of the factory environment. Even though I knew it would not be easy, I had to get off that particular treadmill. I had never really enjoyed the work because working on an assembly line was such a mindless job, but with my work ethic I still had to give 110% effort. I did appreciate the money I earned, but I knew I had to do something else. I just didn't know what. Looking back, this was where I set another goal. The goal was simple: to get a job outside of the factories, no matter what it was.

Peeling Onions

The first non-factory job I had was working for a guy named Byron Hoyt, who owned a restaurant. This restaurant had a few tables, a long bar with stool seating, and the cook prepared the burgers and fries on a grill behind the bar. My job was doing whatever Mr. Hoyt needed me to do. One of my duties was to sweep and mop the place every evening at closing. This was no big deal for me because I had learned to sweep and mop at an early age when my mother was working and I would babysit my brothers. I actually used to enjoy cleaning the house. I guess I like to be living somewhere that's kept nice. I did all sorts of jobs in the back room of this restaurant, and although I don't recall everything I did, I do remember peeling and slicing a lot of potatoes.

I also vividly recall peeling and slicing onions, with tears running down my face. The onions were definitely not the highlight of my restaurant career. Even today, if I can get out of slicing an onion, I will. Compared to the factories, the pay was lower, and it certainly was not a glamorous job by any means, but it was a welcome relief from the rote work on an assembly line. The main thing for me was that it was a change of direction.

When you're feeling stuck, such a change is always positive—it gets you out of the rut and shakes things up. Even if it proves to be the wrong change, it is still a positive step; after all, once you're in motion, changing direction is much easier. Although I was glad to be out of the factories, I could not envision this job becoming a career. I was still on the lookout for something better. I was always aiming higher.

The Postal Service Job

There was a large post office down the street from the restaurant, where their parcel post trucks were located. One day I decided to talk to them, and they offered me a job picking up mail in the downtown area. When I told Mr. Hoyt that I was leaving, he asked me to stay, offered me a raise, and said he would teach me how to cook so I could have a better job than peeling onions and sweeping the floor. I really appreciated his offer, and it taught me that by giving 110%, my work would be appreciated and could lead to a better position. However, in this case, I felt the post office was a step up the ladder. I had to take it.

The post office job was actually fun work, and I enjoyed my time there. I carried a large bag on my shoulder and went into the downtown buildings to pick up mail from the mail chutes. I would load the mail into my mail bag, sling it over my shoulder, and then carry it to deposit into the large outside mail boxes for the mail trucks to pick up later in the day. Then it was on to the next building. The job kept me active, and mostly outside; plus a perk was I got to flirt with the elevator operators in the buildings. During those days, there were no automatic elevators; every single one was operated by a pretty girl. So, I would occasionally take a ride in the elevator hoping to make a date.

After working this position for a while, I heard about some openings for parcel post truck drivers, so I applied and was fortunate enough to be awarded one of those jobs. This was also a fun job, as well as an increase in pay. I had to learn my route and be sure to load the packages in the order I would deliver them so I could get through the route on time. Nothing was computerized the way it is with the package delivery companies today; I had to do the sorting myself—manually. While I liked this work, and the pay was good, I still felt I needed something better if I was going to get what I wanted out of life. Up to this point, all of my jobs had been what I would consider blue collar work, and it was at this point that I decided I needed a job that would offer more potential, more opportunities. However, the first such job that I looked into was more than a little off-putting.

My First Brush with Real Estate

With my new goal in mind, I scanned the Help Wanted ads until I saw an advertisement for a real estate trainee. That sounded promising, so I went to talk to the company. It turned out the reason they were recruiting was they were doing a lot of work in what they called "transition" neighborhoods. They were getting people in white neighborhoods to sell their homes to black buyers. But this wasn't about integration, and the Civil Rights Act of 1968 was still a long way off. By scaring white homeowners into selling—by playing on their prejudices and fears around having black neighbors—the company would acquire properties at a depressed price and then sell the homes to black buyers at an inflated price. This just didn't sit right with me. Once the company owner had explained the deal to me, I saw that I couldn't be involved in this because it was so devious, unscrupulous, and unfair to both the white sellers and the black buyers. I couldn't imagine my black friends from grade school and high school being treated this way.

I'm thankful that I had positive experiences with the black kids who became my friends early in my life and during high school, because, although I had really wanted that real estate job, when I understood what the company was doing, it was very easy for me to say, "*No thanks.*" For a while though, it really set me back. I had to think, if this is what a white collar job is going to be like, maybe I should stay with blue collar work. I now know that the real learning in that situation was that sometimes the route to achieving a goal can carry too high a cost, but the answer is not to abandon the goal, just to find another route.

Insurance Sales

When I did leave the post office, it was for a job as a door to door insurance salesman. I was assigned a route, and on that route I had to collect the weekly premiums. At the same time, I had to make appointments to sell policies to parents with newborn babies. However, I found there were two price lists in the book we carried—one for whites and one for blacks. The black premiums were higher, and when I questioned this, I was told that the actuarial life tables showed that the black population had a shorter life span, so they had to charge a higher premium. While I really wasn't pleased with the explanation, there wasn't much I could do about government-produced actuarial statistics.

I don't remember a lot about this job except for reading the new baby list each morning, and then calling the parents to make appointments to sell them insurance. Making phone calls to mothers of new babies was new to me, but I soon got over being telephone-shy and had some small degree of success. I vividly recall one sad appointment I had with a lady who had just come home from the hospital. I explained the life insurance policy to her with my highly polished sales pitch, and she said okay—she would buy the policy. As I was writing it up, I asked if I could see the baby, and she said, "The baby is still in the hospital." I asked when he would be coming home, and she said she didn't know. *Uh oh!* One of the policy criteria is the baby must be home because that shows that the baby is healthy. Not only was this new mother worried about her baby in the hospital, but because of the rules, I was not allowed to write the insurance policy.

Similar to the restaurant job, I knew that insurance wasn't going to be a long-term job, but it was another stepping stone forward toward my goal. I had to continue to aim higher.

Chapter 6 – Travis Family Origins

I've already said that family is something I really value, and about 20 years ago I did some investigation into my branch of the Travis family tree. It's a fascinating, and frustrating exercise trying to trace family beyond the members personally known. Like most genealogical research, mine soon benefited from similar work done by others in the past; namely Major General Robert J. Travis, who published a family history in the 1950s, tracing the family back to the first immigrants from England to Virginia in the seventeenth century, and even as far back as the Norman Conquest of England in the year 1066. My own personal research was a little closer to home.

The Appalachian Trail

My great-great-great-grandfather John Travis left the Virginia area to travel the Appalachian Trail around 1794. He was the first Travis in this line to immigrate to Tennessee, and I imagine in doing so, he had a clear vision of his goal of providing a much better life for his family. In order to achieve that goal, he was prepared to take enormous risks. Traveling the rugged and dangerous Appalachian Trail was a perilous undertaking. Many lives were lost on that trail.

John was a hard-working farmer, and his children and grandchildren all remained in that Tennessee area as farmers until my father's generation. It was during this time that small farmers were getting more competition from large farming companies, and the children of that generation also wanted a better life. They saw the possibility of that life in the automobile factories that were beginning to expand.

In Tennessee, I was fortunate to share information with Jack Bowker of Dickson County, who had done a tremendous amount of research on the local branch of the Travis family. Through Jack, I was able to locate the burial places of my second and third great-grandfathers, although for John Travis and his wife, Damaris, my brother Bob and I were never able to find and identify the exact grave site. A freeway had been constructed, and the cemetery was in the freeway median, which was a wooded area about 500 feet wide, and ran for miles. A family living nearby told us the general location of the cemetery, and we knew it would be tough to find, but we wanted to give it a try. Bob and I took a rake and shovel and braved crossing the busy freeway to get to the median—with cars speeding past us at about 75 miles per hour.

We searched on three different occasions, but were never able to positively identify the site. We located some possible burial spots where there were large rocks that may have been used as grave markers, and part of a wire fence that may have been used to protect the cemetery. But there were no markings whatsoever. We finally decided that we had probably found the cemetery, but since it was over 200 years old, and in a very remote area, we would never be able to identify the actual graves. Besides, since we were risking our lives every time we crossed that freeway, we though it prudent to be satisfied with the information we had.

I credit the hard-working farmers in my history for passing down their work ethic to me. I believe it also got passed on to my children because they all work very hard in making their living. I like to believe that, among my ancestors, there were visionaries and goal setters who were willing to take extreme risks, and endure great hardships, to realize their dreams and achieve their goals.

Travers

The Travis family name has been traced back to the Norman Conquest of England in 1066. In his book, *The Family of Travis or Travers and Its Allies*, General Robert J. Travis wrote:

> *"The Battle Abbey Roll names one of the chiefs in the Norman army—a companion of William the Conqueror—as 'Travers.' Having taken part in the Battle of Hastings, Travers went on to seize Tulketh Castle, near Preston in the North of England and later married Alison, the daughter and heir of Tulketh and the Travers family lived at Tulketh for centuries."*

During 1666, in search of a better life, William Travers III and his wife Rebecca Booth were the first in our line to emigrate from London to Isle of Wight, Virginia. Somewhere along the way the spelling of the name Travers was changed to Travis.

Col. William Barret Travis

Colonel Travis was one of the defenders of the Alamo, and is my second cousin four generations removed, which put another way means my second great-grandfather would be his second cousin of the same generation. In other words, one of his grandparents was a sibling of one of my great-great-great-great-grandparents, and I am four generations younger than he. Still confused?

Each time I see one of the Alamo movies, I think I see some common Travis family traits. Colonel Travis stuck to his post and died for his cause, but that same steadfast streak could cause the occasional altercation, such as the one with Jim Bowie at the Alamo. I would go so far as to say that the Travis family seems to be highly dedicated to getting a job done, but also a bit stubborn. My wife would agree with the stubborn part.

Brigadier General Robert F. Travis

General Travis was another flier, so obviously I feel some sense of kinship—and we are related. He is a fourth cousin, two generations before me. He was a famous World War II pilot and commander in the Eight Air Force 41st Bombardment Wing, who led 35 combat missions over Nazi-occupied Europe. Sadly, General Travis died in the crash of a B-29 shortly after take-off on August 5, 1950, at Fairfield-Suisun Air Force Base, California. The aircraft was carrying a MK-4 atomic bomb; luckily without the uranium core.

This is the account of his crash according to the USAF Accident Report Summary:

> *"Just prior to lift-off, the number two engine propeller malfunctioned, and the aircraft commander ordered the number two propeller be feathered. After lift-off, the pilot actuated the gear switch to the up position, and the gear did not retract. Due to the increased drag (feathered number two engine and the lowered gear), the rising terrain ahead and to the left, and the inability of the aircraft to climb, the aircraft commander elected to make a 180-degree turn to the right, back toward the base. Upon completion of the turn, the left wing became difficult to hold up. The aircraft commander allowed the aircraft to slide to the left to avoid a trailer court. A crash landing was imminent as the altitude of the aircraft was only a few feet above the ground.*

The aircraft struck the ground with the left wing down at approximately 120 mph. All ten people in the rear compartment were fatally injured. General Travis and one passenger in the forward compartment received fatal injuries; all other crew members and passengers escaped with only minor injuries. About twenty minutes after the crash occurred, the high explosives in the bomb casing ignited. The blast, felt and heard over 30 miles away, caused severe damage to the nearby trailer park and on base."

On October 20, 1950, the Fairfield-Suisun AFB in California was renamed Travis Air Force Base.

In 1962, while I was flying cargo for Zantop Air Transport on their military contract, I made my first flight to California where I landed at Travis Air Force Base. It was winter time when I made this trip, and it was snowing back in Detroit where I was based. When we crossed over the majestic snow-capped mountains surrounding Lake Tahoe, and continued toward Travis AFB, I was amazed at all of the green grass there. It was still winter time, but the grass was emerald green. I was tired of shoveling snow, so when the opportunity to go with Pan Am came in 1966, and I had a choice of being based in New York or San Francisco, it was a no-brainer; California, here we come!

It was heartening to me when I learned that the first airport that I flew into in California, Travis Air Force Base, was named after a relative of mine. Perhaps some of the same genes that were passed on to General Travis by our closest common ancestor, Dr. Edward Travis (1691-1740), were also passed on to me.

Chapter 7 – The Army Years

In November 1953, I received this infamous letter:

Order to Report For Induction
The President of the United States,
To: William Travis
"Greeting:*

Having submitted yourself to a Local Board composed of your neighbors for the purpose of determining your availability for service in the armed forces of the United States, you are hereby ordered to report to the Local Board named above at..."

*(Yes, the President really did say "Greeting" and not "Greetings"!)

The Korean War ended with a ceasefire on July 27, 1953, but the draft was still in progress. When I received the draft notice, I was working for the insurance company, fairly content in my job, and was dating Dee, my wife to be. Obviously, it was with mixed emotions that I received that notice. On the one hand, like other 20-year-olds, I was happy to serve my country. On the other hand, I didn't want to leave my family and girlfriend to start a new life in the military. But there was no choice. Uncle Sam had sent for me, so on December 23, 1953, I reported to Fort Knox, Kentucky, for basic training.

When we, the draftees, arrived at Fort Knox on a bus that cold

December morning, we were immediately assigned to platoons consisting of about 30 men each. The sergeant in charge of my platoon met our bus and immediately started shouting orders at the top of his lungs—which quickly got our attention. His name was Sergeant Bruno, and he let us know right away that he had fought in a combat zone during the early days of the Korean War. They must choose platoon sergeants who are hardened combat veterans, completely devoid of fear, the meanest of the mean, and toughest of the tough, because Sergeant Bruno represented all of that. He was only five feet, eight inches tall, but the way he stood—proud and tall—he appeared to be at least six feet tall. He weighed about 190 pounds, all muscle and, as we would soon learn, would not hesitate to get in the face of the biggest and seemingly toughest of the draftees. From the moment we first encountered Sergeant Bruno, we knew basic training was not going to be a walk in the park.

Sergeant Bruno was so tough he would make the tough sergeant on the TV commercials look like a wimp. If a soldier got smart with him, he would be in his face faster than a light wave on steroids; and if he kept it up, the sergeant would take his shirt off, throw it on the floor, and say, "Come on outside, smart ass, and we'll see who is the toughest." No one, not even the biggest and baddest of the soldiers in our platoon ever took him up on it.

Sergeant Bruno was in control.

Sergeant Bruno learned that I played drums, and said if I bring them when I come back from leave, I could keep them in his room. The platoon sergeants had their own room in the front of the barracks, so I brought the drums down and would play them in his room at every opportunity. As a quid pro quo, for allowing me to bring and store my drums, I had to play the snare drum for our marching drills. We not only did marching drills, we did a lot of calisthenics including jumping jacks, pushups, and pull ups; you name it, we did it.

When I was drafted, I weighed 125 pounds; when I got out of basic training eight weeks later, I weighed 135 pounds. I was whipped into shape fairly quickly by eating a lot of food and gaining muscle tissue from the required exercises. I was proud that I gained ten pounds. Today I would be proud to lose ten pounds.

I did not adjust well to the military, probably because, like the rest of the new soldiers in our platoon, I was disappointed to learn that we would not be going to Korea. If they didn't need us, then why draft us? We didn't even know where we would be stationed after basic training, although we were told that it would not be overseas—it would be somewhere in the United States.

Near the end of our eight weeks of basic training, Sergeant Bruno lightened up, and we were able to see his more human side. He was actually a great guy, and although he didn't show it early on, he had a lot of compassion for his fellow man. He was dedicated to his work and did his job well. He made soldiers out of a bunch of undisciplined, rag tag, young civilian kids from all walks of life, many of whom previously balked at authority. We were taught to respect authority, and if we didn't already know how, we learned to say, "Yes, sir" and "No, sir." I'll always remember Sergeant Bruno because he made a man out of me.

3rd Armored Tank Division

After completing the first eight of the 16-week basic training course, I was assigned to the 3rd Armored Tank Division at Fort Knox for the second eight weeks. Our barracks was next door to the Fort Knox Army Band rehearsal hall, which gave me an idea. I decided that I would be much happier in the army band than in an army tank, so I went over one day and asked what I had to do to get in the band. They said I had to take an audition; since they could use another drummer, they scheduled me for the audition later in the same month.

So, I practiced reading the music they provided me, in the little free time I had, and in a couple of weeks I went for my audition—but I didn't make the cut. Neither my reading nor playing skills were up to their requirement. But that didn't discourage me. It showed me where I was weak, what I needed to work on. It caused me set a new goal, which was to work harder to get into the army band.

Knowing what I had to do to get in the band, I began to study and practice as much as I could. In addition, I would go watch the band rehearse at every opportunity, so I could learn the music they were playing. I even started to visualize myself playing in the band at a concert. This was helping to program my subconscious mind to guide me toward my goal. I could set the goals and visualize myself in that position, but I would not magically achieve that goal. I'd have to work hard at it to gain the skills while my subconscious mind helped guide me there. I was determined that I would somehow get into an army band, so I continued to work hard at gaining the necessary skills.

Now, here's a small insight into how the army works. The draft was for two years, but an on-base recruiter told me that if I reenlisted—which would extend my service from two years to three years and three months—I would have a better chance of getting accepted in the band. Well, how's that for army recruitment? I had already learned that the requisite for getting into the band was simply passing the audition! But I did it anyway. I really wanted to get into an army band, so in April 1954, I reenlisted, extending my stay to three years and three months. I wanted to take advantage of every avenue available to me, and even if it didn't help, there was an upside—a monetary bonus attached to reenlisting. I could always use the money.

The tanks were dirty and muddy, with cold hard metal inside that hurt every time I bumped up against the wall. They were also very loud. We had to learn to maintain them, clean them, drive them, and shoot the gun, as well as serve as the tank commander. The only real fun was driving that big monster, and firing the gun. I subsequently learned that the gun wasn't very accurate, at least not when I was firing it!

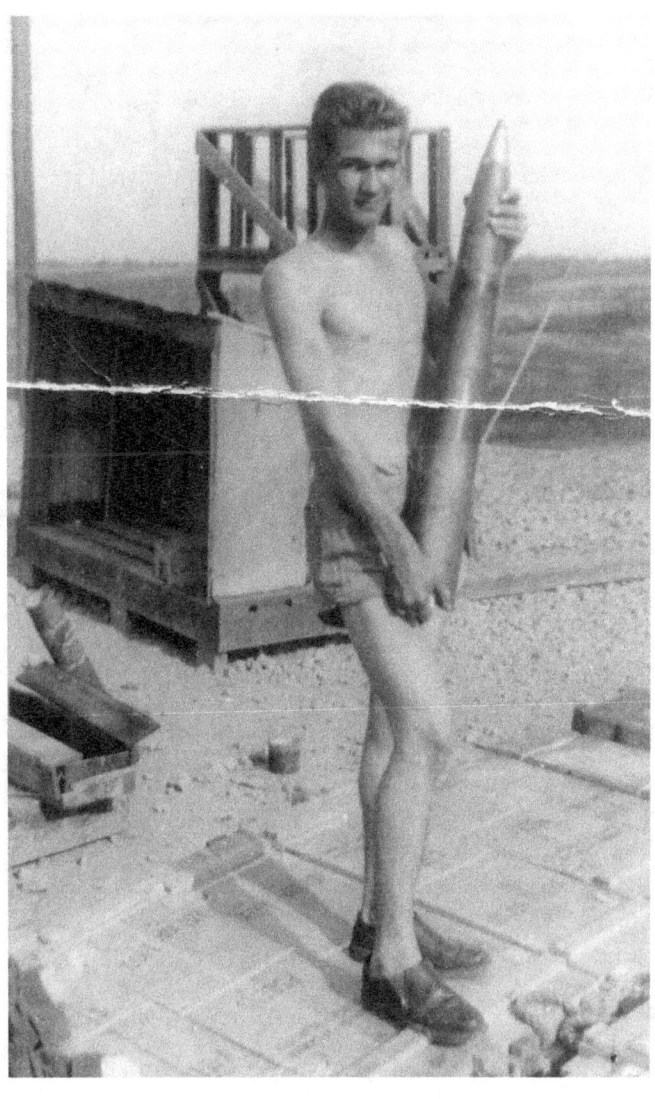

When the tank training was complete, I was sent to Fort Hood, Texas, where I was assigned to the newly reactivated 4th Armored Division. Yep, I was going to be a tank driver. But that was not what I wanted to do. I had been practicing drums a lot, working toward my goal of getting into an army band, so the first thing I did after arriving at Fort Hood was head over to the 4th Armored Division Band office as fast as I could, to request an audition. I had been practicing very hard, hoping for another opportunity. Fortunately, I got the opportunity, and this time I passed the audition. The visualization, goal setting, and hard work had paid off; they helped me achieve my goal. Now, instead of being a tank driver, I was a proud member of the 4th Armored Division Band.

The 4th Armored Division Band

Yes, goal setting along with a lot of hard work does pay off. Believe that. If I had not set the goal, had not done the visualization—which programmed my subconscious mind—and had not worked hard at practicing and learning the music, then I might never have gotten in the band. I didn't know it at the time, but this was one of the major milestones in my life. If not for that goal, I would have been driving tanks, and almost certainly not flying airplanes, because I would not have met some of the people in the band who would later become a huge influence on my life.

The band was immersed in music eight hours a day. We had rehearsals for our concerts, our marching band, and a 17-piece dance band. The marching was brutal; we had to march for long periods of time in the boiling Texas heat. But we were young and became accustomed to it. We also learned to drink a lot of Coca Cola. We had a Coke machine in the barracks, filled with those green curved 6.5 ounce bottles.

Instead of drinking water when we came from marching drill, we would hit the Coke machine where the Coke in the bottle was so cold it was half ice. Although it wasn't good for us, it really tasted refreshing after we had been baked completely dry under that hot Texas sun. It was as if we were addicted to Coke—we weren't interested in water. We only drank water when the Coke machine was empty. The only thing I would have enjoyed more would have been a half-frozen RC Cola with a Moon Pie, like we used to have each Saturday on the farm.

Photo by: U.S. Army Photographer – Calvey

Navy Music School

As part of that musical immersion, the army gave me a very special experience: I was selected to attend the U.S. Navy School of Music for six months in Washington D.C. from January through June, 1955. The school was established in 1935 and was initially run by the U.S. Navy Band. Since 1951, they would invite a small number of army musicians to attend each year. This was a highly concentrated six months of study where drummers had to learn all of the percussion instruments, play in several types of bands, and take music theory classes.

Apart from all things musical, I also learned that the food served to navy personnel at this school was far superior to that served in the army.

I was given ten days to drive to Washington and report to the navy school assignment. That was more than enough time, so I drove to Detroit first, where Dee and I could get married.

We couldn't afford a big wedding, and we had very little time, so

Bill and Dee Wedding Photo

the next morning after I arrived, we drove three hours to Angola, Indiana, where we could do all the paperwork and get married by a Justice of the Peace on the same day.

Two days later I had to be on my way to D.C.

Dee remained in Detroit to tie up some loose ends, while I got settled in at the music school. For the first month I lived on base in D.C., and soon Dee was able to join me. Before she arrived, I had rented a small apartment in a house near the base that was divided into several one bedroom units. We had a room upstairs that was a combination bedroom and living room, and a postage stamp kitchen. We shared the one and only bathroom, which was located in the hallway on the second floor, with another newlywed couple whose room was next to ours.

It was an enjoyable time for us. Dee took a day job; we did some sightseeing on the weekends, and went to small jazz clubs to hear some of the top jazz musicians who were playing around town. I recall seeing one of my favorite jazz drummers, Shelly Manne, and a young pianist, Pete Jolly, who was nominated for a Grammy Award in 1963. Bill Haley and the Comets rock and roll group was only a couple of years old when I got to see them perform in D.C. The navy music school assignment was a fantastic musical education experience, and I got to spend a lot of time with my new wife.

They say the service changes people, and it does. But the biggest change to my life, while I was in the army, was entirely unconnected to the military—it occurred when I married Dee. After our navy school assignment, Dee moved with me to Texas where we rented a small three-room house off base. A year later she gave birth to our first child, a fantastic son, Arthur. This made me a more responsible person because now I had a duty to support my family. After leaving the army, we were blessed with three lovely daughters: Sandra, Connie, and Katrina.

Soon after returning from the navy music school, I became the drummer in our 4th Armored Division 17-piece dance band. This was a significant move for me. Not only did I meet and play with some people who had a real influence on my future life, but later—after Pan Am—I went on to have my own 17-piece dance band that played for weddings and private parties in San Francisco.

Gene Bruhjell: Flying Lessons

While I was learning to be a husband and a dad in Fort Hood, I also managed two other major turning points, and these were linked to being in the army. I got serious about education, and I took my first flying lesson—which hooked me for life.

One of my drummer friends in the 4th Armored Division Band, Gene Bruhjell, was an avid reader. Seeing him read caused me to become interested in reading again. After I started reading, I became interested in finishing my education. At the time, Gene was also taking flying lessons at a small airport in Temple, Texas, about 30 miles from the base. After talking to Gene several times about what he was doing, I went with him to take a lesson myself. That first flying lesson got me hooked, and I credit Gene with being a major force in my becoming an airline pilot.

In the 1990s, after I retired from Pan Am, I would sometimes play for a Dixieland band, the Jasstown Revelators, with leader Jim Hubbard and his wife and band manager Sherry Hubbard, when their regular drummer, Bob Stover, wasn't available.

On this one Saturday, we were playing an all-day Dixieland Jazz Festival near San Jose, California. The festival had several rooms for different bands, and in each room there were different bands rotating each hour. Ed Zimbrick and his 10th Avenue Band were going to be playing just prior to our set.

Bill with Jasstown Revelators, Photo by Dee Travis

When the 10th Avenue Band started playing, I noticed that the drummer looked familiar. I kept staring, and within a few minutes I realized who he was. I said to Dee, "That's Gene Bruhjell, my old army buddy, the drummer friend of mine from the 4th Armored Division Band who got me interested in flying."

Dee said, "Sure, I remember Gene."

We could hardly wait until they finished playing so we could say hello and invite Gene to join us for lunch. When the 10th Avenue Band finished their set, Dee and I went to say hello, and later, after our Jasstown Revelators band finished playing our set, we had a memorable lunch with Gene.

We had lost contact with all of our army friends after being discharged, so we had a lot of catching up to do in a short period of time. I told Gene that because he introduced me to flying all those years ago in a little Piper Cub in Texas, he had been instrumental in me becoming a Pan Am airline pilot, and I wanted to take this opportunity to let him know what he had done for my life.

We had an interesting conversation over lunch, reminiscing about the old army days, and I think, given how things turned out, Dee had forgiven Gene for taking me flying that first time. It was nice to have the opportunity to give Gene the credit he was due, for being such a huge influence on my life.

Ed Zimbrick has been the owner and president of the successful real estate franchise, Century 21 Alpha, in the San Jose area since 1975, and still finds time to travel and perform with his highly popular and successful 10th Avenue Band. They perform all over the world, playing at Dixieland festivals and swing dances, and are booked up to one year in advance. Gene toured with them for a long time.

However, the last time I saw the band, there was a different drummer. He told me that Gene had a massive heart attack on board an

10th Avenue Band at Roman Coliseum Photo Courtesy Ed Zimbrick

airplane while traveling to one of the band's gigs, and the plane had to make an emergency landing to get him to a hospital. Recently, I learned that Gene had recovered from that heart attack and had been playing in bands in the Phoenix area up until his death in 2010, at the age of 78.

When I took that first flying lesson with Gene, it cost $5.00, which in 1955 was a lot of money. Dee was so furious, she cried. As a wonderful mother and careful homemaker, Dee understood the need to save money, so it was natural for her to be upset when I took the flying lesson.

I love that Dee is frugal and good at saving money, and I hate that I'm prone to spending. She's always saving up for something, and sometimes forgets she has it saved. Saving money is a wonderful habit she learned when she was young.

To earn extra money, and to play jazz and dance music outside of the army band environment, Robert Ashley, Rick, Triplet, Rod Gress, and I formed a dance combo to play at local clubs several nights a week. For a night's playing, we each earned $5.00. I was spending a full night's earnings on a flight lesson that, given our circumstances, must have seemed pretty frivolous. But we finally were able to rationalize the flying lessons because it was using money that I worked extra for in the dance combo—not money from my army salary. Dee has always been an inspiration, very supportive of my dreams, and continues to offer constructive criticism to keep me in check—like she did when I took the flying lessons.

First Solo

The small grass field airport was located in Temple, Texas, just 30 miles from our Fort Hood base, so Gene and I didn't have too far to go to take the flying lessons. To my surprise, I felt right at home in the Piper Cub. It was exhilarating, a real feeling of freedom, to be in the air even though it took a lot of work and concentration to fly the plane. At the time, I didn't think about becoming an airline pilot; flying was just something that I recognized I had a knack for. I was good at it, learned it fast, and enjoyed every minute of the flying experience. There was a lot to learn from the *Private Pilot* handbooks, but I enjoyed learning about flying as much as I did the actual flying.

One day, on my ninth lesson, the instructor and I went around the flight pattern, making one touch-and-go (that's a landing followed by a take-off without coming to a complete stop), and as we went around again, he said, "Make a full stop landing this time." When we stopped, he opened the door, got out, and suddenly I was on my way to my first solo flight. The first solo was quite an experience; I knew I could do it, but I was anxious. I suddenly realized that if I screwed up, I was on my own. There was no one to back me up. I was now in charge of my own destiny. The instructor that I'd counted on to back me up for the past eight one-hour-long lessons was safely on the ground, looking up at me. I had been kicked out of the nest.

Now it was time to spread my wings and fly, to soar like an eagle—alone.

Several years later, after I became a flight instructor, I learned that the instructor also got anxious. *I feel he is ready, but did I turn him loose too soon? Will he be okay? Will he be safe?* All of those thoughts go through the instructor's mind, mirroring what's going on in the student's mind up in the air.

The weather was absolutely perfect on this day. The winds were light and the only clouds in the sky were high and scattered. The Piper Cub is a very forgiving airplane, making it an easy airplane to fly, and to land, once I got the hang of landing on two front wheels, then allowing the tail wheel to touch down. I felt that I had learned my lessons well. And, thanks to good weather, an easy-to-fly Piper Cub, and an excellent instructor—my first solo went well. After soloing, I didn't fly too often because we needed to conserve what little money we had.

While I wasn't thinking about being an airline pilot at the time, the Piper Cub flying experience set the ground work for what was to follow. Therefore, I believe it was my subconscious mind at work, guiding me through the flying experience, on the way to helping me achieve my ultimate goal of having a white collar job making $10,000 per year.

GED and Early Discharge

I'm not sure I ever saw Gene Bruhjell without a book unless he was playing music or flying. While he probably didn't realize it, he also got me interested in reading. Once I started, it almost became an obsession. I don't recall many of the books I read at that time because it was so many years ago, but I do remember getting through some psychology books, including Sigmund Freud. Once

I started learning under my own steam, as it were, my thoughts turned back to a formal education.

Some of the members of the 4th Armored Division Band were highly educated, and with me being a high school drop-out, I really respected those individuals. They were also great musicians whose musical skills far exceeded my amateur abilities—I felt honored to have them as good friends. It was because my friends were highly educated, as well as talented, that I finally realized the need to complete my education so I wouldn't be relegated to a life in the factories after being discharged from the army. That made me start to think about what more I should do in order to reach my long-term goals. I began to think about taking the GED test as the first step, in order to earn my high school diploma. Then I could decide where I should go from there.

GED Test

One day, while I was in the band office checking on how to get access to the GED test, I noticed that that our office clerk had been promoted to sergeant; he was junior to me. Since rank was typically awarded to those who were senior, I wondered why I hadn't received a promotion. Was I being passed over for some reason that I wasn't aware? Obviously, I was concerned. So, when I left the office, I went to ask the band commander, Chief Warrant Officer Hal Gibson, why I didn't also receive a promotion, since I was senior to the clerk. He told me the clerk learned that there was one rank available at the division level, so he applied for it, and got it.

Well, I didn't think that was the way it worked; I believed the commander gave out the ranks and thought he was probably just doing a favor for his clerk. However, I was not about to question the band commander, or I might never have gotten a promotion. But being the good guy that our Mr. Gibson (as CWOs are addressed) was, he promised that I would get the next sergeant rank available. He kept his promise; the rank came within two weeks. That promotion in rank from corporal to sergeant was more than welcome because it involved a well needed pay raise, plus a little more prestige.

During the time I was studying for the GED test, I learned that I could apply for an "early out" in order to go to college. I knew that I needed to go to college in order to better myself and have any chance of achieving my long-term goal of having a white collar job and making $10,000 a year, but I didn't know what college courses to pursue.

The thought of getting a degree in percussion and working in recording studios crossed my mind; studying business also entered into the equation. I finally decided to attend a junior college to take the academic courses with an emphasis on business. But before I could apply, I had to pass the GED test. Studying for that test then became my short-term goal and primary focus. I studied for about a month because I did not want to flunk that test. Failure was not an option. I had to pass that test.

The long awaited day finally came. I took the test, and to my surprise, the test was relatively easy. I also realized that it was probably easy because I had devoted the necessary time to study hard for the test. Had I not applied myself in the preparation phase, then the test may have been hard. Obviously, I was proud of my achievement. Now that I had been issued my High School Equivalency Diploma on May 23, 1956, I could apply for college. During the rest of the year I was busy making plans, getting the necessary papers from the army to go to school, and applying for enrollment. On January 28, 1957, three months before my scheduled discharge date, I received my early Honorable Discharge, along with six cents per mile automobile allowance to drive the 1,300 miles from Texas to our home in

Detroit. That was a grand total of $78.00, which today will do little more than buy one tank of gas. Back then, at about twenty cents per gallon, that was plenty. We were happy to be on our way back home to Detroit to try and make a new life for our family.

As I look back on how things had begun to take shape over the years, I find it interesting how the subconscious mind works, how decisions are made, and how one may not realize why they're being made until they look back, as I'm doing, later in life, when they see the pieces of the puzzle having come together. Now, I can look back and see all of the short-term goals being realized, taking me ever closer to realizing the long-term goal. It's like climbing a ladder, one step at a time.

Many years later, I realized that being drafted into the army—while not welcome at the time—was one of the best things that could have happened to me. The army taught me discipline, and it allowed me to become friends with some highly educated and talented musicians like Robert Ashley, Gene Bruhjell, and others—who lifted me up. I learned the responsibility of being a husband and father, and I made the decision to get my education and pursue higher goals.

Had I not been drafted into the army, I may have fallen back into my old practice of hanging out with my factory friends and ending up back in the factory work environment—never to get out.

Chapter 8 – Pursuing the Dream

Lolo & Siria

When I got out of the army and we moved back to Detroit, I got to meet Dee's parents for the first time. Dee was also the child of a family who migrated to Detroit. Her mother, Siria, was of Mexican descent, born in Texas. She had moved to Detroit to accompany an older sister who was a professional dancer in a Mexican entertainment and dance troupe that performed throughout the country.

Her father, Lolo, was Spanish, born in Spain. It was around 1930 when Lolo immigrated to Detroit because he heard there was work to be had in the factories. He was looking to make a better life for himself, and subsequently, went to work for the Ford Motor Company.

Early in 1933, at a friend's party in Detroit, Lolo and Siria first met. They fell in love, and Siria elected to leave the dance troupe to marry Lolo and make a life with her husband in Detroit. Dee was born the following year.

Lolo lived long enough to meet his grandson, our son Art, and was able to spend some time with us after I got out of the army. He was of an earlier generation who believed that people should marry within their own nationality. So, naturally, he was a little concerned that his daughter had married a "gringo." However, he warmed up to me very quickly, welcomed me into his family with open arms, and we became good friends.

College

In chapter seven I mentioned that on January 28, 1957, I received my early Honorable Discharge and headed back to Detroit to go to college. I didn't know what I wanted to do for the future, but I knew I had to go to college, so I enrolled in the Henry Ford Community College in Detroit to study business, which was of tremendous value later on when I ran various businesses while still flying for Pan Am, and after retirement.

Despite enjoying the business studies, I still felt the pull to do something involving music, so during the first semester I talked to Wayne State University to see if I could transfer there to major in percussion. I thought I would like to work in the music studios in New York or Los Angeles. I had started to play some weekend gigs to make extra money because I didn't have an income, which I needed now that I had a family to support. My parents allowed us to live with them during this time because I couldn't afford to rent a place to live, go to college, and have time to study. I would have had to go back to working evenings in the factory, with very little time to study.

When I spoke with the counselor at Wayne State, she told me I could not enroll there with percussion as my major because I didn't have three years of piano study. I had played piano without formal lessons for one year, and played vibraphone in the Navy Music School for six months, but that didn't fulfill the requirement. What she didn't tell me—and I'm forever grateful because I know now that I was a better pilot than a musician—is that I could have enrolled with a major in music and taken all the percussion classes I wanted, and continue the piano study. The most important factor in being able to work in the music studio is not a college degree—it's ones playing ability.

However, since I didn't know I would be able to get the percussion education I felt I needed, I elected to drop the idea of becoming a professional musician. The other option would have been to go on the road as an itinerant musician by joining one of the territory bands. Those bands traveled a circuit of several states, playing one or two-nighters for several months at a time. Since I had a propensity for alcohol, and many musicians were into drugs, I decided that working with a territory band would not be a wise choice for me. The pay was not that good, and I felt there was a risk I could succumb to alcohol and drugs and lose my family. Therefore, a music career was finally ruled out.

One of my classmates was interested in flying, and, like me, he had taken a few lessons. He was considering becoming an airline pilot, but had yet to make up his mind. At this point, I had never consciously considered becoming an airline pilot; however, I was intrigued by the possibility. I enjoyed the fifteen hours I had flown in the Piper Cub, and flying seemed to come fairly easy to me. So, he and I did some research into what it would take to become an airline pilot.

During those days of no computers and no Internet, researching a career opportunity was not easy; so, as we brainstormed, we came up with the idea of going to the airport to see if we could talk to some airline pilots and get as much information as possible. After that brilliant idea, on several occasions we went to the Willow Run Airport in Ypsilanti and talked to as many pilots as we could, in order to learn more about the job and how to go about getting the flight hours.

From the pilots we spoke with, we learned that it was necessary to have several ratings and licenses. To get a job as an airline co-pilot, I would need Private and Commercial Pilot Licenses, an Instrument Rating, a Multi-Engine Rating, and a couple thousand hours of flying experience. To fly as pilot in command (captain), I would need an Air Transport Pilot Rating; that would come later. In the meantime, I was becoming more interested. I was beginning to see that if I succeeded in getting into aviation, it could fulfill my dream and goals of having that white collar job, and earning $10,000 per year.

But now there were two questions to be answered. First, how to get started? Second, how would I pay for the training?

Flight Training

As part of my research on how to get started, I went to the National Flying Service in Westland, MI.—a small grass-field airport in the Detroit suburbs that operated a flying school. There I discovered the answers to both my questions.

The school had a good reputation, and they had an arrangement with a loan company to finance the flying. It was also approved for GI Bill training; just what I needed. The government would allow one change of education program, which meant I could change from college to flying, but if flying didn't work for me, I could not change back. But when I made the decision to change, I knew there would be no turning back. Aviation was going to be my career.

The GI Bill would only pay 75% of my flight training up through the Commercial License. That license allowed one to fly for hire as a commercial pilot. Any training beyond that, such as the Instructors Rating and Multi-Engine Rating, would have to be fully paid for by the student.

By entering into this program, the flight school would allow me to fly as much as I wanted to, plus take the ground training. At the end of each week, the school would bill the government for their share, and the loan company would loan me the money to pay the school for my share. While the interest rate was high, the advantage of being able to fly as much as possible meant that it would take fewer hours to get the license, thereby costing less money overall. Getting the license sooner meant that I could go to work sooner, which was a huge advantage.

It took several years to pay off the loan, but it was worth every penny of interest I paid.

Financially, these were tough times for my wife and me. When I started flight training, our second child was on its way, and I felt the need to get my family out on our own. My parents' home was small, and adding my wife, our son, me, and a soon-to-arrive daughter in the small house made it uncomfortable for everyone. Consequently, I started working evenings in a factory so I could afford to make the loan payments on the flight training, and pay for trailer park space for a small mobile home that Dee's father subsequently bought for us.

Although it felt good to be out on our own again, it was difficult; we now had to shoulder the extra expenses of having this small mobile home. We had to skimp on groceries—no sweets, only the necessities. We couldn't even afford to buy meat, and eating out was never an option. My parents realized this, and sometimes they would buy meat and some extra groceries for us.

I was determined to get out of the factories and stay out, but sometimes, when chasing that big dream, I knew I'd have to take a small step backward before taking a big step forward.

I would schedule my flight training in the morning so I could have time in the afternoon to study before going to work at the factory. I started playing weekend gigs again, and many of them were at a night club with a Latin music quartet. The owner wanted to keep the customers drinking instead of keeping them on the dance floor all night, so they required us to play for twenty minutes, and then take a twenty minute break, to give the customers plenty of time to drink and order another round. The club couldn't make money if the customers didn't drink. I decided to take advantage of those twenty minute breaks by taking my flight training books along to the gig. During the breaks, I would sit on the floor in the coat room and study. That way I wouldn't be interrupted, or be tempted to have a drink.

Working and studying sixteen hours a day wasn't easy on the family, but I knew that I had to give 110% to this project if I expected to succeed. I had discovered that I really loved flying, and I was good at it, so this was the career I had to have. Once again, failing was not an option. I had to study as hard as I could.

Within seven months, which was very fast, I was able to earn the Commercial License. With the financial arrangement, I was able to fly more often, and the more I flew in a short period of time, the more I retained. Consequently, I was able to accomplish more in a smaller number of hours.

I was determined to build a solid foundation for my flying career, so I pushed on to get the Instrument Rating, which allowed me to fly in low ceiling and visibility conditions called "Instrument Flight Rules" (IFR)—even though that meant borrowing more money from the loan company. I had to pay the entire cost of getting the Flight Instructors Rating; the GI bill only covered up through the Commercial License. However, I was learning instrument flying at the same time, so the Instrument Rating flight test and the Commercial License flight test were taken simultaneously, saving me a lot of time and money.

Next, it was time to get the Flight Instructors Rating, so that I could teach. That would help me build up the flight time necessary to be able to apply for an airline job. This rating was tough. It required working with an instructor, who would act as my student, and the instructor would make all of the expected student type mistakes, from which I had to recover. At the same time, I had to study for the written part of the rating test. Each license and rating required both a flight test and a written test. But I was determined and completely focused on my goal. Within a few months, I had my Flight Instructor Rating.

Flight Instructor Years

Within a year after starting flight training I had my first job as a light airplane flight instructor. All those long hours of study and juggling jobs had finally paid off. National Flight Service—where I did my training—hired me part-time to supplement the two full-time instructors they already had. Of course, most of the students were assigned to the full-timers, but I was able to get enough work to keep increasing my flight hours and my experience, although not enough to quit my factory job. I was mostly teaching students for their Private Pilot License in a two-seater Aeronca Champ, a tail wheel airplane. The other two, more experienced instructors worked with the advanced students, and rightly so.

One day, I went to visit a friend at Detroit Metro Airport where I learned that Bentley Air Service needed a full-time instructor. I wasted no time in applying for the job and was hired right away. The owner, Mr. Bentley, had a full-time job elsewhere and was only there part of the time, leaving the running of the operation to a manager named Mr. Peck. Mr. Bentley did some instructing, but mostly did operational work around the school, leaving the majority of the instructing to me and the other full time instructor. The emphasis was on in-flight training, not ground training. Detroit Metro was a large airport with a control tower; therefore, the students had to learn to fly out of a controlled airfield by communicating with the tower and flying at the same time. It was much more demanding on both the instructor and the student than flying out of the grass field at the National Flying Service.

We also flew occasional charter flights at Bentley's. Sometimes, a customer would want a quicker and more economical option than the larger commercial airlines, and they preferred to charter our Cessna 182 for a short trip. Bentley had all tricycle gear airplanes—such as the Cessna 152, 172 and 182—and they were a lot more comfortable to land than the tail wheel airplanes in my last job. Students would start out in the 152, and later be checked out in the 172 and 182. The 172 was a good airplane for doing instrument work because it had the full instrumentation; the 182 was good for charters, and advanced students who wanted to take a cross-country trip and carry some guest passengers with them.

Going to work for Mr. Bentley turned out to be a good decision for me. I was working full time, getting a lot of experience, and building up flying time which was required for my ultimate goal of going with the airlines. And for the first time, I was able to leave the factory jobs permanently—never to return.

While at Bentley's, I met some very interesting people. One person who chartered our Cessna 182 quite a lot was film executive William Deneen. At the time, he was Vice President of Film Production for Encyclopedia Britannica, and later, the founder of the Learning Corporation of America. I flew a lot of charters for Bill in the Cessna 182 when he needed to go to meetings, and he took a few lessons from me so he could do some of the flying en route. One charter was to Chicago to visit another senior executive for Encyclopedia Britannica. To my surprise, I was invited to stay at the executive's home and have dinner with them at an upscale restaurant that evening. It was a good feeling because I was treated like a friend, not like a staff member who would not be allowed to socialize with the executives.

On another occasion, I flew Artie Fields, a brilliant musician and music-commercial producer with whom I worked night music jobs fairly regularly, to Chicago. He was going there to dub a Chicago-based vocal group's voices into a commercial, where the instrumental music was already recorded.

Artie was an innovative composer. One day he recorded the machines building the cars at the Chevrolet factory, and then orchestrated them into a mechanical symphony playing the song, "See the USA in your Chevrolet"—the song (a 1950s TV commercial) was made famous by Dinah Shore on her "Dinah Shore Chevy Show." For a time, Artie also worked on the Dinah Shore Chevy Show as the orchestra leader.

There was a famous race track announcer, Jack Riggs, who announced at the dog racetracks in Florida during the winter, then announced at the Detroit horse racetracks and other tracks around the country during the summer. He came to Bentley's because he needed someone to teach him to fly the small airplane he had recently purchased. I spent several hours teaching him to fly his airplane over a period of days, and one day he invited me to visit him in the announcer's booth at the racetrack where he worked.

We became good friends and I would visit him at the racetrack at every opportunity. I was amazed at his memory; when the horses came out on the track, he would go through the race card verbalizing the horses' and the jockeys' names and colors. He would go through the list twice; and then as the horses were getting into the starting gate, he would go through it one more time. By that time he had all the names and colors memorized so he could call the race from memory, looking through his binoculars for the entire race. During the race there was no time to look at the card; he had to have all the details memorized before the race began.

Instructing was a great way to really learn to fly. Getting the licenses and ratings taught me how to fly the airplane, but instructing took me to a different level, by expanding my skills. I had to allow the student enough leeway to make mistakes—because they learn from their mistakes. However, I couldn't allow the mistake to get out of hand because it could cause the student to lose confidence, or in the worst case, an airplane could get damaged, or someone could get injured. My ability to monitor everything in and around the airplane, and be able to allow the student to make mistakes, greatly increased my skills as a pilot.

Multi Engine Rating

Mr. Bentley, Doug (another instructor), and I decided to buy a multi-engine airplane in order to get our Multi-Engine Ratings. The airplane was a two-engine Cessna T-50 called the Bamboo Bomber, which had a wood and metal frame covered with fabric. Because I needed a Multi-Engine Rating, but didn't have the money, my parents loaned me $500 to pay for my share of the airplane. It took us a couple of months to replace the old, frayed fabric, making the airplane airworthy again, but when that job was complete, we were able to embark on the more exciting project of flying our two-engine beauty. Mr. Bentley had his Multi-Engine Rating, so he was the instructor for Doug and me. Soon, with Mr. Bentley's generous help, Doug and I were able to get our Multi-Engine Rating.

We used the T-50 as a charter plane until the following year when it was time to have the annual FAA check. Apparently, the FAA inspector assigned to this inspection didn't want the airplane operating, because it was all fabric, so he wouldn't do a complete inspection. He pointed out an item that needed to be repaired, and wrote in his report that when this was repaired he would do another inspection.

By doing the inspection in this piece-meal manner, we had no idea what the final cost to renew the license would be, so we were pretty much forced to give up the project and sell the airplane. We found a vintage airplane collector who was happy to buy the Bamboo Bomber from us, at a discounted price.

But the Bamboo Bomber had served its purpose: I had my Multi-Engine Rating, and with two years of instructing on my resume, it was time to begin looking for my first airline job.

Chapter 9 –
The Zantop Air Transport Years

Across the hangar from Bentley's was an air cargo carrier, Zantop Air Transport, which was owned by the three Zantop brothers. They operated a small fleet of C-46 airplanes and flew automobile parts to and from the Detroit automobile factories. As they grew, they were awarded contracts with the military Logistics Air Command, commonly called "Logair." One day, I decided to go to their office to apply for a job, and although they were not hiring at the time, they said they would call me in about three months when they expected to be hiring.

The day finally came; I received a phone call from Gene Zerkel, the Zantop chief pilot, asking me to come for an interview. Gene was a tall man with a tough, stern personality, and he did not mince words.

"Bill, I have your application in my hand. Are you still interested in a job?"

"Yes, sir, I am."

"Then come to my office at ten o'clock tomorrow morning."

"Yes, sir, I'll be there at 10:00 a.m. sharp!"

I made a point to be there the next morning at exactly ten o'clock, and when I arrived, the secretary immediately took me into Gene Zerkel's office. Gene was a very imposing figure. I actually felt a little intimidated by him. Possibly that was no accident; it was easy for Gene, with his stature, to tower over people. He was very abrupt, and the interview only lasted about five minutes. He had my application in his hand as he asked me several questions. After the questions, he finally said,

"Bill, what are you looking for in a job?"

"I'm looking for job security, sir."

I had worked at factories where there was no job security. You always expected a pink slip when it was time for the next year's model change. After receiving the pink slip, you really didn't know if you would be recalled after the changeover.

Gene said, "What do you mean job security?"

"Well, I would like to have a permanent job where I don't have to worry about getting laid off twice a year. It's too difficult to support my family when I keep getting laid off."

"That's fair enough," said Gene. "Now here's what you need to do. Go downstairs and get on the airplane with the two other new hires to do three take-offs and landings so you'll be qualified to fly the airplane as co-pilot. When that's finished, come back up here and you'll get three hours of ground school. Then you'll report tonight at 9:30 p.m. for an 11:30 p.m. flight to Saint Louis."

"But, Mr. Zerkel, I have a student scheduled in two hours. I can't do this today. I need to give notice to Mr. Bentley."

"Do you want the job?"

"Yes, sir, I do."

"Then get your ass outside and get on that airplane or you won't get the job!"

I knew this was a serious ultimatum that required me to make a split-second decision. The job was the chance of a lifetime. I had been working toward this goal for my entire life; if I turned down this opportunity, I didn't know when, or if, I would get another one. Mr. Bentley knew that I had applied to Zantop, and I had told him that I had this interview appointment. He also knew that instructing was a stepping stone toward an airline career. My problem was I didn't like to burn bridges. On the other hand I badly needed this job, and felt that I needed to put my family and career first, so I hoped Mr. Bentley would understand.

I didn't turn it down.

I said, "Yes, sir." Then I started to go downstairs to get on the airplane, but first I asked to make a quick phone call to get another instructor to substitute for me. Gene said, "Okay."

Zantop C-46 photo courtesy of Bob Garrard

The Three Bounces

The training ride to get three take-offs and landings really turned out to be a case of having three new hires ride through one take-off and landing each, by just sitting in the co-pilot seat and following the controls while the captain flew the airplane. That means we were instructed to place our hands lightly on the control wheel and keep our feet off the rudder pedals. We did get to handle the controls and fly the airplane while we were in the air, but not for the take-off and landing.

The C-46 was a tail wheel airplane with a huge fuselage and tail and rudder assembly which makes it a very difficult airplane to land in a crosswind. Once a pilot learns to land this airplane in a cross wind, he can land anything in those types of conditions. For a new hire that has flown nothing larger than a Cessna T-50, just finding the ground with the C-46 was a difficult task. This instructor, who was a check captain for Zantop, was not about to risk letting us new hires attempt to land that airplane and possibly ruin his day.

On paper, each of us had three take-offs and landings which qualified us to fly the C-46 as a co-pilot. Then we went inside for three hours of ground school. I can't say that I learned much in those three hours because there was so much information crammed into it. My head was still spinning from the interview with Zerkel, the situation with Bentley, and the three bounces. But at the end of the class we were supposedly ready to go.

The First Flight

That evening, I reported a little earlier than the nine-thirty report time. By being early, I could have more time to do what I had to do—although I didn't know what I had to do. I began to look at the paperwork the operations clerk gave me, and remembered, vaguely, how to do the weight and balance form. So I began to work on that.

When the captain, Luther Smith, came in, I introduced myself and let him know that I was completely green and needed all the help I could get. It was common during those days that when working for a non-scheduled airline the training would most likely all be on-the-job. Captain Smith had logged thousands of hours flying the C-46, and was more than capable of flying the airplane all by himself, so the fact that I was a greenhorn didn't seem to bother him at all. He just smiled and said he would teach me how to fly this old crate.

After the paperwork was completed, we went to the airplane where Captain Smith showed me how to do a pre-flight inspection. When the aircraft was loaded, we started the engines and were on our way. I should say *he* started the engines, because I didn't know how. I had seen the check pilot start them, but he didn't tell us what he was doing.

When we left Detroit on these flights, the airplanes were fully loaded; at times, it would seem like they were more than fully loaded. This time was no exception. We had taxied heavily into position on the runway when Metro Tower said, "Zantop 452 cleared for take-off."

"Roger Metro, Zantop 452 cleared for take-off."

At least I knew how to talk on the radio!

We were on our way; my first flight as an airline co-pilot. To say I was excited would definitely be an understatement. Captain Smith pushed the throttles forward, set the throttles at take-off power, and then made a quick check of the engine instruments to see that the engines were functioning properly. We slowly started lumbering down the runway, so slow that I wondered if we would reach lift-off speed before the end of the runway.

I began worrying about the load; were we too heavy to take off? Would we have to abort the take-off? I quickly glanced over at Captain Smith, who didn't seem to be worried at all. His demeanor was calm, cool, and collected. After all, he had logged thousands of hours flying the C-46 airplane; he knew exactly how it would perform under different loads and in various weather conditions. He had confidence—and it showed. That made me feel more comfortable.

We finally reached lift-off speed; the captain pulled the plane off the ground, and when we were safely airborne, he called, "Gear up."

I had seen the check pilot pull the gear up, but he had not allowed the students to do it. It looked easy enough, so I reached down and placed the lever in the palm of my left hand, pushed the lever in, then reached my thumb around to release the lever latch so I could pull the lever up, which would raise the gear.

Damn! My thumb wouldn't reach the lever latch. What the hell would I do now? Just as I started to bring my right hand over to move the lever latch while holding the gear lever in with the left hand, the captain reached over, knocked my left hand off the gear lever, and pulled the gear up himself.

OHHH Shit! My first flight and I couldn't even get the gear up.

The overloaded C-46 struggled out over the end of the runway with the gear coming up, and we were finally able to climb on up to our cruising altitude of 6,000 feet without further incident.

After we leveled off at cruise altitude and had some time, the captain laughed about the incident. He said that was not unusual. He showed me that instead of hitting the lever with the palm of the hand, which causes the thumb to not be able to reach far enough forward, that I should strike the lever at a position on the middle joint of the fingers, not the palm of the hand. Then the thumb can easily reach the lever latch. It's certainly easy enough—once shown how to do it properly. Not being able to get the gear up, however, was just my first mistake.

We arrived at Saint Louis, and as we were taxiing to the cargo area, Captain Smith asked me to cancel our flight plan.

"Yes, sir." I changed the radio frequency to Saint Louis radio and said, "Saint Louis radio, this is Zantop 452, please cancel our flight plan."

"Zantop 452, we don't have a flight plan on file for you."

"Okay, thank you."

The captain said, "Is it cancelled?"

"Yes, sir, it's cancelled," I replied.

I didn't intend to lie about it. However, I didn't want to discuss it while taxiing to the cargo terminal. When we were in the cargo office doing the paperwork for the return flight, I told Captain Smith that there was no flight plan filed, that I hadn't known I was supposed to file one, and that I was simply over my head, having had almost zero training. He said, "No problem, kid, you'll be okay." Luckily, since the flight was a VFR flight (visual flight rules), no flight plan was required by the FAA. However, it's always advisable to file a flight plan, and it was required by the company.

Because Zantop was growing very fast, a pilot could check out as captain as fast as he was capable. However, Zantop would not turn a new captain loose without being properly trained and being assured that he could do the job. The pilot also had to pass an FAA check ride in order to be allowed to fly as captain. But, however demanding, making captain was my next goal.

It took me two winters to get myself ready. Learning to fly the plane and being able to handle it in all conditions and emergencies was the easier part. The captains were constantly training us co-pilots, and their willingness to help us advance was a tremendous help. Dealing with the weather, however, was where I needed more experience.

The Detroit climate made the ability to deal with bad weather essential. Some of the situations I had to be able to handle included flying in the vicinity of thunderstorms without weather radar; preventing the aircraft from stalling when ice accumulates on the wings, disrupting the airflow; and landing on snow or ice without sliding off the side or end of the runway. The only way to learn those skills was through experience.

The first winter, experiencing these weather conditions for the first time, I would sometimes think, *what the hell am I doing here? Right now I wish I were off this damn airplane and out of this rotten weather.* As brand new airline pilots, we co-pilots were probably as scared as any passengers would be, except we were sitting up front having to deal with the weather head on, and having to learn to make the right decisions. But it was an essential learning experience.

The second winter was better because we knew what to expect; we were better able to plan and begin to make our own decisions. As part of the training, the captains would ask us how we would handle a situation that we were about to encounter. Having us do the thinking—forcing us to make the decisions—was a very effective training technique.

My First and Second Major Goals Realized

It was during the summer of 1961, after two years with Zantop, that I earned my Air Transport Pilot Rating and checked out as captain. I had achieved my first goal. Now I could say that I had a real white collar job.

However, there was still the second major goal I had yet to achieve: earning $10,000 a year. During 1961, I earned $9,931.72. Close, but not there yet. But, in 1962, I finally realized that second goal when I earned $11,495.02. I had done it! If I could achieve those two goals—which seemed so impossible when I first set them—I had to ask myself, *what else can I do?*

At that time, my immediate goal was to fly as much as I could in order to make more money to better support my family. That said, after I checked out as captain, the thought was in the back of my mind to eventually get hired by a major airline. I didn't know who that airline would be because they hired at different times. I would just have to be ready, get there at the right time, and hope I had the right amount of experience. Getting hired by a major airline was going to be my next big goal.

As Zantop expanded, they bought four-engine DC-4 and DC-6 aircraft. I wasn't senior enough to fly the DC-6, so I set my sights on the DC-4, eventually checking out as captain on that aircraft. Next on my list was the Argosy, a four-engine jet turboprop aircraft. I managed to check out on the Argosy and fly it for three years before I was hired by Pan Am. However, the Argosy almost proved to be my undoing. I had an accident in the Argosy that almost cost me my career, sending me back to the factories.

The Incidents

The accident in the Argosy wasn't the first piece of bad flying luck I had while I was with Zantop. In 1962, after I had some captain experience under my belt, I was on a C-46 flying to and from Warner Robbins Air Force Base, Georgia. My co-pilot was a very experienced pilot who would go on to check out as captain himself the following year. I have to admit I've forgotten his name, so I'll call him Bob.

The cargo they loaded on the C-46 at Warner Robbins was large paper rolls. They were six feet long, twelve inches in diameter, and very heavy. The C-46 had a tail wheel, so there was quite a downward angle from the front to the rear of the cabin. The loading crew loaded the rolls on so that they were lengthways across the cabin, which meant that if they were to break loose, they would roll to the back of the cabin.

When I expressed concern with the manner in which the cargo was being loaded, the load master assured me that the rolls would be tied down securely, with no chance of coming loose. Well, famous last words. They weren't going to be on the airplane with us. Reluctantly, I accepted the load. The cabin wasn't completely bulked out, but with the heavy cargo and the fuel load, we were at maximum take-off weight.

It was the co-pilot's turn to make the take-off, and I was handling the radio communications.

"Zantop 215, this is Robbins tower cleared into position and cleared for take-off."

"Roger Zantop 215, we're rolling."

Bob pushed the throttles forward and we began rolling down the runway, slowly gaining speed. As we reached the appropriate speeds, I called out, "V1"—before this speed the pilot would abort take-off if there is a problem; after reaching that speed, they could continue the take-off. Then I called, "Vr"—the rotate speed, which is when the pilot lifts the nose to start the climb.

At Vr, Bob lifted the heavy airplane gently off the runway and called, "Gear up." As I raised the gear lever, starting the landing gear retraction, I heard, and felt, an unusual thumping sound. I thought it might be coming from the landing gear, but the gear was retracting properly.

Just then the aircraft starting porpoising; the nose was going up and down and the yoke was going back and forth. I grabbed the yoke and yelled to Bob, "What the hell are you doing?"

"It's not me, Bill, it's the airplane," came the reply. Now we were lumbering out over the tree tops, just barely gaining altitude. I finally realized that the thumping noise had to be the load of paper rolls breaking loose.

"Bob, I have the airplane; go back and see what the hell is happening."

In a few seconds Bob yelled, "Bill, the rolls broke loose and they're at the rear of the cabin."

"Start moving them," I yelled, still lumbering dangerously close to the tree tops, trying to keep the airplane at an airspeed that would keep us from stalling and falling out of the sky. I was still using full power to keep the airplane from stalling, and almost full forward elevator to compensate for the extra weight in the aft cargo area. Using full power for too long can cause both engines to fail. Even one engine failure at this point would be disastrous.

"Robbins Tower, Zantop 215 has an emergency—need to proceed straight out."

"Roger, Zantop 215, do you need assistance?"

"Yes, from God. Our load broke loose and the co-pilot is trying to move it. We'll get back to you"

"Roger, Zantop 215, you are cleared straight out; let us know what we can do."

I could tell each time Bob got another roll moved forward because I would get a slight increase in airspeed, and a little gain in altitude. Another roll, another few knots of airspeed and a few feet of precious altitude.

Thank God for adrenaline; Bob called on every ounce of strength he had, and more, in order to quickly get those rolls moved to a position where we could finally gain airspeed and altitude. I credit Bob for saving our lives that evening because he summoned up super-human strength and speed. When he got back into the cockpit, he collapsed from exhaustion for about an hour.

"Robbins Tower, this is Zantop 215, we have the problem under control now and are proceeding to Detroit. Cancel the emergency and thank you for your assistance."

"Roger, Zantop 215, it looks like God gave you a helping hand. Have a safe flight to Detroit; contact departure control on 132.7."

"Roger, Zantop 215, goodnight."

The Argosy

After four years with Zantop, having flown the C-46 and DC-4, the opportunity to fly the Armstrong Whitworth Argosy AW 650 came along. This was a four-engine turboprop airplane—a jet engine with a propeller. The training was excellent; we had instructors from the Armstrong Whitworth factory in England as our ground and flight instructors.

The engines were manufactured by Rolls Royce and were known to be very reliable. Nevertheless, there were precautions taken during the engine start process. The instructor pointed out a metal flap in the cowling of the engine, saying that in the rare event of an engine fire on the ground during engine start, the fire guard, who would be standing on the ground, would insert the nozzle of a CO_2 fire extinguisher inside the flap, to quickly extinguish the fire.

The flap was about six inches by six inches square. It had the words "Rolls Royce" conspicuously printed in large bold letters on the flap. The instructor pointed out that the flap had an emergency system, whereby, in the unlikely event an engine did catch fire, the flap would automatically rotate 180 degrees to prominently display the words, Pratt and Whitney!

The Logair (Logistics Air Command) military contract required the Argosy to be based in Wright Patterson Air Force Base in Dayton, Ohio. For one year I commuted to Dayton; then we were able to buy our first home there, so my wife and three children could relocate to Dayton with me. Our fourth child was born in Dayton, a few months before I was hired by Pan Am.

The flight schedule at Wright Patterson was a pilot's dream. We would fly one route up the east coast to several military bases, remain overnight at Boston, then return home by dinner time the next evening, sometimes bringing lobster home for dinner. The following day we would leave in the morning, fly to Warner Robbins, and then back home the same day. Another route took us up around northern Michigan and back on the same day.

Our home was about a mile to the west of the runway, inside the downwind leg of the traffic pattern, so when we flew back to Wright Patterson, the home was located on the left side of the airplane. I could see it as we flew the downwind leg of the approach. The family knew about what time we were due to arrive, so they would be in the backyard watching for us; I would tip the wing to say, "Hi, I'm home." The kids would then get ready to hit the swimming pool as soon as I got home. Flying a schedule where I could be home most of the time was unusual, and highly desirable. I got to spend a lot of time with my family, thoroughly enjoying all of our time together.

The Argosy was built especially for cargo. The cockpit sat on top of the cabin, and we had to climb a ladder to get up there. The large front and rear doors of the airplane swung open, making it fast and easy to load the cargo using forklifts. The cargo was tied down on pallets in advance, and then a forklift would lift the pallets and place them on rollers that ran the full length of the cabin. The cargo handlers would then push the loaded pallets into place and lock them to the floor to prevent rolling. Our flight engineer would usually be in the cargo cabin supervising the loading to make sure we could depart on schedule. Keeping on schedule was important because it was one of the ways the military measured Zantop's performance.

Belly Landing

On August 26, 1964, Co-pilot Richard Mlynarek, Flight Engineer Lowell Bright, and I were flying the northern Michigan route and had landed in Wurtsmith AFB. From there we were to proceed to Selfridge AFB and then home to Wright Patterson.

When we were ready to depart Wurtsmith, the airplane had a light load. The manual showed that we could take off on a 3,500 foot runway with that load. The runway at Wurtsmith was 11,800 feet long, which was more than sufficient. The weather was light winds, unlimited visibility, and clear skies, so we expected a routine flight to Selfridge. However, it turned out to be anything but routine. We never left Wurtsmith, and if Mr. Blackwood of the Federal Aviation Agency had had his way, Zantop Air Transport would have fired me, and I'd have lost my flying career.

The Vr (rotation) speed was computed to be 96 knots. As the flight engineer started the engines, I placed the flap handle to 12 degrees as per the procedure taught by the Armstrong Whitworth flight instructors. When the flight engineer read the checklist and called out, "Flaps," I visually checked that the flap handle was set at the 12-degree indent, and the flap indicator showed 12 degrees. The co-pilot concurred.

From our position on the cargo ramp we were cleared onto the high speed taxiway, and then cleared for take-off. A high speed taxiway allowed the aircraft to begin to accelerate before reaching the start end of the runway because there were only a few degrees of turn, which could be done at high speed.

Dick Mlynarek called V1, then Vr. At Vr, I rotated the aircraft. It came off the ground at approximately 100 knots with the nose feeling a bit heavy as we rotated. Dick then called out V2, which was the safety climb speed. At the V2 call, I pressed the brake pedals to stop the wheels from rotating and called, "Gear up." Shortly after Dick raised the gear handle, the aircraft began to porpoise. (This was much different from the porpoising I had experienced on the C-46 when the load of paper rolls broke loose.)

We had probably climbed to 25-30 feet when the nose made a couple of gyrations, each increasing in intensity. The last one had the nose pointed down such that I felt if it went through another gyration, we could have crashed nose first into the runway. As the nose came up from that gyration, I eased the throttle back and put the aircraft on the ground, on its belly. We had lifted off the ground at approximately 2,500 feet, landed on the belly at approximately 3,500 feet, and then skidded until we came to a stop at about 6,200 feet down the runway.

I can tell you, in situations like this, a pilot doesn't have much time to run through their options. *Do I try to fly the aircraft out of this situation? Do I put it back on the ground? Which is the safest option? If I try to fly it out of this situation, I may succeed, but if I don't succeed, then I could crash and kill my crew members, and possibly kill someone else on the ground.*

When split-second decisions like this are made, the brain processes the options at the speed of light, like an ultra-fast computer computation, only faster. The safest option, in my opinion, was to put the aircraft back down on the runway. That was what I did. No one was placed in danger and no one was injured.

After stopping, our main concern was the possibility of fire. We shut the engines down, and Lowell, the flight engineer, immediately went downstairs to check for fire, hoping there'd be no need to use that flap on the engine cowling that the Whitworth Armstrong instructor had joked about. Fortunately there was no sign of fire. The co-pilot and I followed. After we all got out of the aircraft safely, we went to inspect the damage.

The nose gear had not completely retracted. Consequently, there was some damage to the nose wheel doors. The Argosy was a high wing aircraft; so fortunately, there was no damage to the main gear, or to the engines. The bottom of the body, however, had some damage from skidding on the concrete. Due to the relatively minor damage, this belly landing would have been considered an "incident," but later it was discovered that one spar, which is a structural member of the aircraft frame, had damage. That damaged spar changed it from being an incident, to the more serious label as an "accident." Now I had an accident on my record—the nightmare was about to begin.

All hell broke loose on the base because our Argosy had caused Wurtsmith AFB to shut down their only runway, causing the base commander to be extremely upset. They had fighter jets in the air that had certain scheduled times to land and our accident was interfering with their operation—some of the fighter jets would have to be diverted to other air force bases.

Photo of Argosy after belly landing, by Bill Travis

A civilian airplane had closed his runway!

His attitude was that we should get that piece of junk off his runway—now—before he called out his bulldozers to shove it off the side of the runway. We contacted Zantop headquarters, and they immediately put the wheels in motion to get the aircraft off the runway, and to begin the investigation.

Within two hours of the accident, Chief Pilot Gene Zerkel, Duane Zantop, and two members of the FAA arrived and began extensive questioning with my crew and me about what happened. We were treated with the utmost respect by these two FAA members and Zantop management.

Several days later, a neighbor of mine in Dayton, who was an aeronautical engineer, told me what could have caused the porpoising. The Argosy had a "bob weight" device as part of the elevator control system. He said that it was possible for a resonating frequency to be induced into the bob weight, causing it to begin oscillating. When it starts oscillating, it's difficult to stop.

However, just as Rolls Royce wouldn't want to admit that a Rolls Royce engine could catch fire, Armstrong Whitworth was not about to admit that there may be a fault in the design of their elevator control system. They emphatically denied that the bob weight could have malfunctioned through a resonating frequency build up. There never was a cause of the accident determined. My theory remains with my neighbor, the aeronautical engineer, that it was a fault in the bob weight mechanism.

About 24 hours after the accident (yes, we were still there), Mr. Blackwood, another FAA inspector, arrived to participate in the investigation. That is when things went to hell in a handbasket. This man came in with a pre-determined opinion of what had happened. His opinion was that I screwed up—somehow.

He didn't know how—or even if—I screwed up. Yet, he was determined to place the blame on me.

We met him as he first arrived in the Wurtsmith flight operations room. Instead of going to a private room, as we should have, he began asking questions while we were standing in the operations room, in the presence of a lot of people. His line of questioning in the beginning, instead of being fact finding, was accusatory. He didn't believe what any of my crew told him. He asked if I rotated, then bounced back on the gear and lost control. He asked if I started to make a left turn out immediately after breaking ground, and stalled, or in some manner lost control of the aircraft.

Neither of those scenarios made logical sense.

If I had made a left turn and stalled, we would have crashed off the left side of the runway, instead of doing a smooth controlled belly landing and remaining on the runway center line.

If I had bounced back onto the runway, on the gear, and lost control, then we obviously would not have retracted the gear. The tower operators saw exactly what happened and confirmed that we didn't bounce back on the gear. They also provided written statements as to what they saw.

Then he asked if I knew the feeling of sitting in a chair with my eyes covered, being turned around several times, and then opening my eyes to find that things seem different than they really are. That was his way of saying that I must have gotten vertigo. What was he thinking?

Insinuating that I had vertigo was ludicrous. At that point, I had had enough. I told him that I would not listen to any more of his accusations, nor discuss the incident with him any further, except at a formal hearing, or with an attorney present. Gene Zerkel, who was present while these absurd accusations were going on, asked Blackwood how he would explain that all three crew members would have the same sensation, since our stories were all substantially the same. After that day, the vertigo theory was never mentioned again. However, Mr. Blackwood was still out to try to place the blame squarely on my shoulders. As we concluded the conversation in the operations office, his parting remark was, "If nothing is found wrong with the aircraft then it's going to be called pilot error!"

A week later, after we had returned home, I ran into Lowell and his wife, Alma. She gave me a hug and said, "Bill, thank you for putting that airplane back on the ground. Lowell is sure that if you hadn't, it would have crashed." That made my day. To know that another crew member absolutely believed I did the right thing was a wonderful feeling.

Nothing was ever found wrong with the aircraft that we were aware of. Flight tests were made on another Argosy under similar conditions, but what we experienced could not be duplicated. After the flight tests, Mr. Blackwood proceeded to file a formal complaint requesting my license to be suspended.

Fortunately, the Zantop brothers knew me well; they also knew the co-pilot and flight engineer well. They didn't believe we were lying about what had happened. All three of us were flying a lot of hours, making a lot of take-offs and landings; consequently, we were all very sharp pilots. The company knew that.

Lloyd Zantop made my day when he told me that he would have their company attorney defend me. That was a welcome relief because I would not have been able to afford an attorney to fight the FAA. I would have lost my license.

A few days after returning home from the accident, I received a phone call that I was to be given a check ride by Check Captain John Palmer before I could be placed back on flight status. This was standard procedure. I reported to the Wright Patterson airport at 4:00 p.m. as instructed, but the aircraft wasn't there. It had been delayed. However, Mr. Blackwood was there. He intended to go on the check ride with us. I knew this was bad news because this guy was determined to railroad me any way he could.

The aircraft didn't arrive until 3:00 a.m., eleven hours after my scheduled check ride. We had been waiting at the airport all night. I should have declined to go ahead with the check ride, because I had been up since 7:00 a.m. the day before, and would have been completely within my rights to refuse a check ride under those conditions. However, I had flown with little sleep many times before, and was confident in my ability, so I decided to take this in stride—I just wanted it over with.

While the aircraft was being refueled and checked by the maintenance crew, Palmer, Blackwood and I had breakfast. Much to my surprise, Mr. Blackwood began to give me an oral exam, asking questions about the airplane and its operation, during breakfast. Today, that type of treatment wouldn't be tolerated, but at that time, I felt I had no choice. My job was on the line. I didn't know what might happen if I had refused to take an oral exam during breakfast, or refused the flight check due to fatigue.

During the oral exam, Mr. Blackwood heatedly argued with me that I had done something wrong. He accused me of lying. His demeanor was reminiscent of the old time detectives with the bright light shining directly into the alleged perpetrator's eyes, badgering him until he confessed. It wouldn't matter if he was actually innocent; what they wanted was a confession.

He accused me of not having completed the take-off check list. He insisted that the flaps had come down to the take-off position during the take-off roll, thus causing the porpoising. But I knew, and so did my crew, that the flaps had been set at 12 degrees—exactly where they should have been. Interestingly, when the FAA later revised the charges, they said the flaps must have been at zero. When they couldn't prove one theory, they changed to another.

After this grueling, so-called oral exam was finished, we proceeded to the aircraft to get ready for the inflight portion of the check ride. Check Captain Palmer, who was an excellent pilot with years of experience, and a very fair individual, sat in the co-pilot seat. Mr. Blackwood sat in the jump seat directly behind me. An observer, which is what Mr. Blackwood was, is supposed to sit quietly, just observing, while the check captain directs the pilot being tested to perform the required flight maneuvers.

That was not the way it played out.

Remember: I had had an accident just a week earlier. An aircraft accident, no matter how minor it is, creates a tremendous amount of stress and anxiety on the pilots. Blackwood's obvious agenda was to prove me incompetent so he could suspend my license. That agenda, in addition to sitting up all night at the airport waiting for the airplane, and his grueling me over breakfast, placed me under a lot more stress. Obviously, these are not the ideal circumstances under which a pilot should have to take a potentially career ending check ride.

When the airplane fueling and servicing was complete, we climbed on board and began the check ride. After the first take off, Blackwood stood up, directly behind my shoulders, when he should have been seated with his seat belt fastened, and started continuously asking me questions about what I would do if certain situations arose. All the time he was asking the questions, I was in the process of making a simulated instrument approach with a hood over my head so I couldn't see outside.

This is the part of an approach where all crew members are supposed to be supporting the pilot flying. Yet, this obnoxious inspector leaned over my shoulder trying his best to distract me—trying to cause me to fail my check ride. All that was missing was a bright light shining in my eyes.

Had I failed the check ride, he could say, "You see, Travis is incompetent; that shows that he screwed up at Wurtsmith and lied about it." But I was not about to let Mr. Blackwood mess with my mind to accomplish his agenda. I concentrated on my flying, only answering his distracting questions when I had time.

After the check ride, when he learned that he couldn't rattle me, that I was sharp enough to fly a perfect check ride while performing under extreme pressure, he told Captain Palmer, "I will have to write in my report that Travis carried out his flight check ride as per the operations manual, and that I saw nothing unsafe in his operating practice or handling of the aircraft. However, if I were the company, I would not have him as an employee!"

Captain Palmer, who had been quiet through the entire check ride, except to tell me what maneuvers to do next, finally defended me. He said, "I disagree with you Mr. Blackwood. The Zantop brothers also disagree with you. We feel that Captain Travis is an exemplary employee, and the company is furnishing their attorney to defend him. And, as you have just witnessed, he can fly the hell out of this airplane." With that, Captain Palmer signed the paper releasing me to go back to flight status.

The battle with the FAA continued for over a year. Finally, on November 8, 1965, they sent a letter withdrawing the charges. In part, the letter said:

"...After final evaluation prior to trial, and in consultation with the manufacturer, we have concluded that the evidence is insufficient to establish that you operated the airplane carelessly or that you rotated the aircraft prior to reaching Vr or rotated the aircraft at too high an angle with a resultant loss of speed...."

But wait, that's not all. They had to slap my hand with this nonsense:

"...However, we are officially reprimanding you for your premature raising of the landing gear of said aircraft. While there were references in the Argosy manual to raise the gear after rotation and braking the wheels, these references pertain to the original type procedures and would not be an acceptable customary practice...."

How crazy is that? The Argosy manual was our official operating manual that we were trained on, and must follow. Yet, the FAA stated that the instruction in the operating manual doesn't apply to this aircraft! That was interesting because during the grueling check ride, while Mr. Blackwood was leaning over my shoulder badgering me, I used the same gear raising procedure for each take-off during the check ride. Mr. Blackwood never made a comment about that procedure.

But at least it was over. The "official reprimand" was a futile attempt for the FAA to save face because they were wrong. They wasted a year of taxpayer's money.

An accident stays on a pilot's record forever. Therefore, when I interviewed for Pan Am, and 28 years later when I interviewed with Delta, I had to tell them about the accident at Wurtsmith AFB. Fortunately, I could also tell them about Zantop supporting me by paying the attorney fees for my defense. I had all the documents with me in case they needed verification, but when I said the company defended me, they said that was all they needed to know. I got hired by Pan Am, and later, Delta, thanks to the Zantop brothers and their trust in me.

It appeared that Mr. Blackwood's ultimate goal was to have Zantop violated, which may have resulted in a promotion for him. If he had succeeded in proving that I was incompetent, then he may have been able to convince the FAA to launch a full scale investigation into all of the Zantop flight operations. Although he failed in his first battle with me, he still proceeded, on his own, to go after Zantop.

Caught in the Act

The following information was reported to me by one of my Zantop pilot friends who remained with Zantop in a management position after I left for Pan Am. He said Mr. Blackwood was constantly in their office requesting different types of documents. One day, during lunch hour, he was there when all but one of the office employees were at lunch. The one person remaining in the office stepped out of the room for a few minutes, and when she returned she caught Mr. Blackwood rummaging through her file cabinet.

That was the undoing of Mr. Blackwood.

The office person immediately called the Zantop brothers, whose offices were just down the hall, to report what Mr. Blackwood had been doing. All three of the brothers, along with Gene Zerkel, responded to physically escort Mr. Blackwood out of their building. They told him to never return. He was wise to heed this instruction because the Zantop brothers were tough and fearless individuals who would have kicked him out again—more forcibly—had he returned.

They didn't stop there. I was told that the Zantop company attorney wrote to the FAA, filing a formal complaint charging Mr. Blackwood with violating their privacy by sneaking into their confidential files, attempting to steal them. They informed the FAA that Mr. Blackwood was permanently persona non grata on the Zantop property. They meant it. My friend informed me that he learned Mr. Blackwood was subsequently reassigned to an office in Alaska.

Hired by Pan Am

It was late in November 1965 when I learned that Pan Am was hiring. Consequently, I scheduled an appointment to go to New York on December 6 for an interview. I would also undergo their pre-employment testing. The process was fairly intensive; I was there for three days, at the end of which, Pan Am offered me the job. I had the choice of being based at Miami, starting work there on December

13, or waiting until January 3, 1966, when I could have my choice of either the New York or San Francisco base.

Seniority is everything with the airlines. Flight schedules, vacations, and promotions are all awarded in bids by seniority. Therefore, starting work on December 15 at Miami would have been the obvious choice, considering seniority. It would have meant, however, leaving Zantop without giving notice. After everything the Zantop brothers did for me, I felt I owed them two weeks' notice.

San Francisco was the base my wife and I selected, so I gave Zantop my two-week notice and drove to San Francisco to start work with Pan Am on January 3, 1966. By accepting the January 3 hire date, instead of the December 15 date, I lost about fifty seniority numbers, but it meant I was treating Zantop decently. I didn't burn a bridge unnecessarily. After all, who knows, if I hadn't made it through the Pan Am training, then I could have probably been rehired by Zantop.

Chapter 10 – Pan Am Years, The Beginning

Flight Engineer Training

It was a beautiful California morning. The sky was clear and the temperature was in the low 40s as I drove from the hotel to the Pan Am training facility at San Francisco International Airport. The day was January 3, 1966—my first day of Pan Am flight engineer training. On the way to the airport, I was trying to concentrate on driving in the fast-moving morning commuter traffic, while visualizing myself in the flight engineer's seat flying the line. The idea was to program my subconscious mind to do what was necessary to achieve that goal. In fact, I had spent most of the drive to California on Route 66 doing exactly the same thing. I knew I had to study very hard to achieve that goal, and I was prepared to do just that.

Accepting the job with Pan Am was a risk because I had to leave my family behind in Ohio and pay for lodging in San Francisco during the training, which could take up to six months. This would cause a huge drain on our savings. There was also the risk that if I didn't successfully complete the training, I would lose the job. I was acutely aware that if it didn't work out, I would have neither job nor money.

However, I had a new goal, which was to become a Pan Am airline pilot. Although I knew it was necessary to be aware of the risk, I refused to program failure into my mind. I kept reminding myself that failure was not an option; I kept focusing on what I needed to do to succeed.

I was given the option to start either as flight engineer or as navigator. I chose the flight engineer position for two reasons. The first was a navigator started out at only $500 monthly pay during training, while a flight engineer was paid $1,000 per month. The second was the flight engineer position would teach me much more about the aircraft, and I wanted to learn as much as possible.

I was already looking forward to completing the flight engineer training because then I could move on to training as a co-pilot, since all the flight engineers had to be qualified as pilots on the aircraft. I was eager for the opportunity to actually fly the Boeing 707, my first jet airplane, if only for a few hours in training. After that, I would not be in the co-pilot seat again for two years while I paid my dues as a flight engineer.

Going backwards from flying as captain for five years at Zantop, to sitting in the flight engineer seat was a huge adjustment. The way I was able to get beyond that was to think of the future. The next step would be moving up to first officer (as the co-pilots were called then), and next to the captain's seat. To start with, we expected to be able to check out as captain within five years; but later, as the airline began to lose money, furlough pilots and reduce the number of airplanes, it became obvious that none of us new-hires would be flying as captain in five years. It turned out to be almost twenty years for me. Twenty years in the first officer seat was a disappointment, but the job as a Pan Am pilot was still one of the best jobs in the world—a job that I would not trade for anything.

The first day of training consisted of a lecture on the history of Pan Am, which was interesting, but, in my opinion, a waste of time and company money. It would have been much cheaper to give each of us a few pages depicting the history that we could read at home.

On another day, we had an equally useless lecture which dealt with how we should dress when we came to the airport in our civilian clothes. We were instructed to wear sport coats or suits, just to come to the operations office to pick up revisions or check our flight schedules. We were also instructed on how our wives should answer the phone when Pan Am called. I couldn't get over the waste of time and money those lectures cost. No wonder the training was going to take six months.

Although time and money were wasted, the training was excellent; in fact, in many cases it was overkill. For example, the 707 had an electronic control box that contained components to control various electronic functions on the aircraft; if it failed, there was an alternate procedure. However, there was no access to the box; once it failed, nothing could be done to get it operating again. The box was full of diodes, resisters, transistors, and other devices to route, reroute, and restrict electronic flow from one end of the box to the other.

It's similar to the computer motherboard of today; however, it was encased in a box that we couldn't access. Yet we were required to learn how all the electrons flowed through that inaccessible box. When I started this class, however, I knew absolutely nothing about electronics. I did know that if I flipped a light switch up, a light should go on. If it didn't go on—change the light bulb.

During this phase of ground school training, there were two flight engineers paired with one flight engineer instructor. There were twenty flight engineer students. That meant Pan Am was paying ten flight engineer instructors to do what one instructor could do in a class of twenty students. What were they thinking? Well, I know. It's called job protection. When a company is making a lot of money, the fat will grow. People will build kingdoms out of small departments; those kingdoms will continue growing until management finally learns that they need to get lean, and trim off all that excess fat.

The flight engineer I was paired with had studied electronics in college; he was on top of it all the way. Unfortunately for me, the instructor paced the class to the other engineer's ability, causing me to suffer because of my lack of electronic knowledge. Consequently, I had a difficult time keeping up. I finally had to buy a book on electronics and burn the midnight oil in order to understand what was happening in that control box. It was tough, but I finally caught up and passed that section of the course. The sad thing is that instead of spending a week on that box, it could have taken less than one minute for the instructor to say,

"This is the electronic control box that controls these circuits. It's located in the radio section in the lower 41 electrical compartment; it cannot be accessed or opened. If it fails, read the check list and select the alternate source."

It was that simple. We had no need to know how the electrons flowed through that box. We only needed to know how to use the alternate procedure in the event of a failure of the box.

Part of the reason for this superfluous training is that the flight engineer instructors were professional engineers. They were not pilots. They were a separate entity. They built this little training kingdom and kept it going until someone wised up and realized that this depth of training was entirely unnecessary. Finally, a few years later, they modified the engineer training program so that it focused more on practical, operational matters.

FAA Written Exam

After completing the flight engineer ground training, we had to take an FAA written exam in order to get the Flight Engineer Rating. The exam was on the Lockheed Constellation. None of us had flown, or knew anything about, that airplane. Pan Am said they would either send us to New York to study the "Connie," or we could stay here and take the test on our own. Since I had seen so much wasted time and money in the training department, I thought I would be a good guy and stay in San Francisco to do this by myself, rather than waste more company money by going to New York.

What a mistake that turned out to be. I studied the Connie manual, but it was not comprehensive enough to pass the exam. I failed the first test, and the flight engineer instructor wasn't happy. I studied more, took the test again, and failed it again. Each test had different questions, so the ones I memorized when I took the first test were not on the second test.

At this point, when I told the instructor that I failed again, he said, "Well, if you fail it again, you'll be fired."

I didn't come to work for Pan Am and work my ass off only to be fired. What really bothered me about this instructor's attitude was that I was trying to save the company money by not going to New York, and he was unsympathetic to that cause. The following day, I went into the Chief Engineer's office and told him the story.

I said, "I don't think it's fair for me to be fired when I'm trying to save the company money by not going to New York, and if the policy is to only allow one to take the test three times, without any formal training, then please send me to New York to get the training."

He agreed this wasn't fair. After thinking for a moment, he said, "When Pan Am hires flight engineers who already have the Flight Engineer Rating; they don't know how many times they have taken the test before they came to Pan Am, so we shouldn't restrict you. Therefore, I'll give you the option of taking the test until you pass it, or go to New York."

I told him I felt I was pretty close to passing the test, and would continue to study here on my own as long as I wouldn't be fired if I failed it again.

He said, "Fine, just relax, study, and don't worry. You'll get it."

The next time I took the test I passed it. What a relief.

I didn't program myself to fail, but in this case I made the mistake of thinking more about saving the company money than looking out for my own welfare. I should have elected to go to New York to take the formal training on the Connie when the option was offered. That was a learning experience for me.

Be Aware of Negatives

We need to be aware of negatives so we can avoid them, or take care of them if they arise. I never anticipated that a negative issue such as the FAA written test being on a different airplane than the one we were studying would occur, or that attempting to save the company money by doing the studying on my own would create a problem for me. However, when that occurred and presented a stumbling block, I was able to deal with it successfully because of my goal to succeed.

Similarly, a quarterback will always be aware of the negative aspect of pass rushers coming at him, looking to take him down so they can do the quarterback-sack-dance. He'll make every effort to avoid them, all the while concentrating on the positive aspect, which is the immediate goal of finding an open receiver to successfully throw the ball to.

In flying an airplane, the pilots will monitor the engines' performance through gauges that provide indications of problems, realizing that at any moment they could be faced with an emergency situation. However, they don't dwell on that negative aspect—they simply maintain awareness. After checking the engines' performance, they'll go back to the positive monitoring of the direction the aircraft is heading in, all the while proceeding toward their goal: the destination airport.

Being aware of negatives is absolutely a good thing; we must maintain awareness. However, we must concentrate and focus on our goals; we must not allow the negatives to hold us back. Dr. Maxwell Maltz said in his book, *"Psycho-Cybernetics,"* "Negative feedback will act as a sort of automatic control to help us steer clear of failure and guide us to success."

Flying the Line as a Flight Engineer

June 1966. At last, the flight engineer training was complete. It was time for me to begin flying the line as a flight engineer. At first, I flew a lot of Pan Am air cargo flights because they were mostly flown by those of us with low seniority. By flying these cargo flights that the more senior flight engineers didn't want, I was able to get decent schedules.

But my first priority was to get my family moved out to California. After I flew a few trips on the line, I was able to get enough time off to go back home and drive to California with my family.

Route 66

The moving van was packed and already on its way. After loading the car with our clothes and four children, we started driving down Route 66, anxious to start our new life in California. The kids handled the trip well; but our seven-month-old daughter, Katrina, who was just learning to crawl, was uncomfortable much of the way. Spending several days cooped up in a cramped car takes a toll on the young ones because they aren't able to burn off some of their youthful energy.

We decided it would be a good idea to stop for a day in Las Vegas, staying at the Stardust Hotel, so the kids could enjoy a day out of the car and do some swimming. That evening we hired a babysitter so Dee and I could go out for dinner and a show. The next morning, the kids had another swim, then, it was on the road again, on Route 66, heading toward our new life in San Francisco.

Eventually, we bought a house in Danville, a town where some of my pilot friends lived. Sully Sullenberger—who landed US Airways Flight 1549 in the Hudson River after striking a flock of geese—also lived there. I never met him, although I recently read his book about the experience of successfully ditching that A320 in the water—a feat which saved the lives of all those aboard.

After that first year of flying the all-cargo planes, I started flying the passenger planes because more of the flying was done during the day. It seemed the only time the cargo planes flew was at night. At that time, Pan Am was the largest airline in the world, so in that first year, when someone asked me who I worked for, I would say, "I work for the world's largest fly-by-night outfit."

Aside from making more money as a flight engineer, I did learn much more about the airplane itself. The captain and first officer's job was to fly the airplane, but it was the flight engineer's job to know more about the operation of the aircraft's systems than anyone else.

As flight engineer, the routine was like this: I would report to operations, meet the captain and get a copy of the paperwork, including the flight log, weight and balance, and fuel sheet. I would then proceed to the airplane to carry out my pre-flight inspection. First, I would complete a portion of the cockpit check, and then proceed to walk around the outside of the aircraft, checking the engine intake and exhaust areas for damage, the wheels and landing gear assembly, and then the moveable controls such as ailerons, flaps, and elevators, as well as checking the general condition of the rest of the outside. Finally, I would return to the cockpit to finish checking the instruments, and also check that the correct amount of fuel had been added.

When it was time to start the engines, I would read the pre-start check list. Either the captain or first officer would check the item and respond as appropriate. There would be three sets of eyes checking that each item was in place. While on the ground, and then after we were at cruising altitude, my seat would be facing toward the engineer's panel, which is on the right side of the airplane, so I could monitor the airplane system instruments. During takeoff, the seat would slide up to immediately behind the center pedestal between the two pilots and face forward. From this position, as the pilot making the take-off advanced the throttles forward, I would monitor the engine instruments on the front panel ahead of me, and keep my hands on the rear levers attached to the throttles.

That way, if the pilot rejected the take-off and pulled the throttles back, I would hold them in the rear position while the pilot then pulled the levers on the forward side of the throttles up to activate reverse thrust to help the airplane come to a stop. On landing, it would be similar.

When the thrust reversers were activated, the engines would rev up, sounding like the aircraft was getting ready to take off again; what was really happening was the clamshell doors on the rear of the engines were closing. The exhaust air provided the thrust that propelled the airplane forward. By closing those clamshell doors, and then accelerating the engines, the exhaust air was deflected forward, which provided a reverse thrust condition, causing the airplane to slow down. When the airplane was sufficiently slowed by the reverse thrust, it was then safe to use the wheel brakes to bring the airplane to a stop. Using the brakes at too high a speed could overheat and damage the brake assembly.

In flight, my job as engineer was to monitor and control the pressurization, air conditioning, hydraulic systems, and balance the fuel. There were fuel tanks in the belly of the aircraft and in each wing. The fuel was first burned off from the belly tank and then burned off in the wings in a sequence that maintained a balance of weight between the wings and the fuselage.

A Screw in the Galley

The flight engineer's job also included assisting the flight attendants if they had any galley malfunctions. On a flight to Tokyo one day, because of the long duty day, we had a relief crew; one relief pilot and one relief engineer. I had just left the engineer seat, being replaced by my relief engineer, when a flight attendant came in to ask for help. She was a tall blonde Scandinavian, who spoke very good English, although with a heavy Swedish accent.

She said, "Excuse me, can one of you gentlemen give me a screw in the galley, about this long," indicating with her hands.

Of course the crew was always eager to please, so the captain quickly turned around and said, "That's a job for the captain."

The co-pilot and relief engineer simultaneously uttered that it was a job for them. For a moment, I thought the whole cockpit was going to empty out.

When there was a relief engineer on board, the primary engineer was referred to as the first engineer. Since I was the first engineer, and was standing near the cockpit doorway, I said,

"Any screw job in the galley is the responsibility of the first engineer," and out the door I went to attend to my duties.

There are several ovens in the first class galley. One of the ovens had a couple of screws in the back that had come loose, allowing the oven to shake too much. If the screws were to work completely loose, the oven could fall forward, possibly giving someone severe burns. Those ovens were narrow, about ten inches wide by thirty inches high, and were still hot. She needed a long screwdriver to reach to the back of the oven and tighten the screws. After assessing the situation, I went back to my flight bag, got my eight-inch screwdriver, and took care of the screw in the galley.

One very important thing that pilots needed to understand, and unfortunately some didn't, was that the flight attendants control the food. If the pilots pissed off the flight attendants and didn't provide support when it was needed, they could very quickly be placed at the bottom of the food chain.

But if the pissed off flight attendant accidentally dropped the steak on the floor before she brought it out—there was no need to worry—she would brush it off before serving it. In fact it would have been so clean no one would ever have known it had been on the floor.

Treat the flight attendants well, with the respect they deserve, and a pilot could eat almost as well as the Pan Am First Class passengers.

Chapter 11 – Pan Am First Class Service

Welcome Aboard Pan Am

From the moment you stepped aboard a Pan Am airplane, you would discover that Pan Am offered an unparalleled level of attentiveness. An immaculately dressed flight attendant wearing a jacket and hat, would stand at the doorway and welcome you on board; another would take your suit coat to hang up (and return it to you at your destination); another would be waiting to serve you orange juice as you sat down in your luxurious first class seat; while yet another would offer you a choice of newspapers. Then, you could expect to be pampered throughout the gourmet seven-course dinner. The Pan Am first class service was incomparable.

The first class meal service aboard a Pan Am flight was like dining in a 5-star restaurant, with the standard menus planned by Maxim's of Paris; you could expect the entire dinner service to run about three hours. After a cocktail, dinner would be served, and the typical menu would look something like this:

First Course: Hors d'oeuvres: Culinary Specialties served from the Cart
Second Course: Soup: Clear Turtle Soup with Sherry
Third Course: Salad
Fourth Course: Entree

Fifth Course: Selection of Cheese and Fresh Fruit
Sixth Course: Dessert: Macadamia Nut Ice Cream
Seventh Course: After dinner drinks, mints, etc.

    The entrée, on one particular menu, was a choice of Roast Rib Eye of Beef (sliced at your seat with your choice of rare, medium, or well done), Sautéed Lamb in Madras Curry Sauce, Stuffed Squab with Port Wine Sauce, or San Francisco Bay Shrimps Newburg, each served with Garden Vegetables and Oriental Rice. Sometimes, the dessert could be one of my two favorites: Cherries Jubilee or Peach Melba.
    On some flights you may be offered Dom Perignon champagne and Caspian Sea caviar.
    It isn't mentioned very often in books about flight attendants because the airlines have built up the image of flight attendants as the beautiful, glamorous female, but Pan Am also had a lot of male flight attendants. Some of the male flight attendants had been around for many years, and were pursers (the flight attendant in charge of the cabin crew). When it was time to serve dinner, the male pursers would change into the iconic white dinner jacket, which added ambience, elegance, and sophistication to the already impeccable Pan Am service. It was a treat to watch them in action.
    Pan Am was extremely selective about their female flight attendants, and sometimes recruited only three or four women out of every 2,000 applicants. They were all highly intelligent—most of them spoke several languages—and they looked stunning in their couture uniforms. Over the years, the Pan Am flight attendant uniforms were designed by top designers such as Pucci, Adolfo, and Edith Head.
    During the flight attendant training, they learned how to walk on the airplane, how to turn around gracefully, and how to bend at

the knees to serve someone at their seat. In the early days, they had to wear girdles, and at times were even given girdle checks during their pre-flight briefing.

For many years, female flight attendants had to be single. Pan Am would not hire married or divorced women. Later on, they were allowed to get married, and Pan Am would also hire married women. However, if they became pregnant and showing, they had to go on leave. Eventually that policy was dropped.

There was also a rule regarding the make-up the flight attendants could wear; Persian Melon lipstick and matching nail polish was the required color. Sometimes, the color would clash with the woman's skin color, and if that happened, she would have to get special permission from her supervisor to wear something different.

During the '60s and '70s, most passengers dressed up to fly. Most of the men wore suits and the ladies dressed elegantly, as if they were going out for a night on the town. Flying on a Pan Am airplane during those years was very luxurious and glamorous.

It must be difficult for young travelers today, who are subject to long security lines, cattle car boarding procedures, rude and inconsiderate passengers in their sandals and smelly jogging clothes, being cramped into tiny seats with no leg room, and being thrown a bag of peanuts halfway to their destination, to realize that people used to actually dress up to travel—and they traveled in style.

In the Pan Am First Class section it was not uncommon to be seated across the aisle from a famous actor or CEO of a large corporation, and everyone would be treated like royalty. Flying had a certain cachet during those days. It was also expensive. To provide the luxurious Pan Am service and that wide seat spacing, they had to charge.

I could name over one hundred movie stars I've seen on our airplanes during the early days, including Marlon Brando, Van Heflin,

Laurence Harvey, Hugh O'Brien, Zsa Zsa Gabor, Steve McQueen and his dancer/actress wife, Neile Adams, Anna Kashfi , (who was in *Mutiny on the Bounty* with Marlon Brando and later became his wife and mother of his children), and Nick Nolte (who played a gotcha on me, which I'll explain in Chapter 18, in the section about Greenland.) The list goes on and on. They loved flying on Pan Am because of the elegance and the glamorous service.

William Hewlett and David Packard, co-founders of Hewlett Packard (HP), were on board often, as were Hall of Fame Joe Namath, and Jay Leno, before he gained national prominence on the Tonight Show. I would be remiss if I didn't mention the beautiful Maureen O'Hara. While she was never on my airplane, she was married to a famous Pan Am pilot named Charles Blair, and quite often she would accompany him on a flight.

Chapter 12 – Checked Out as a Pan Am First Officer

Life was good. After two years in the flight engineer seat, my seniority finally allowed me to check out as a 707 first officer. It wasn't exactly where I wanted to be, but I was one step closer to that coveted left seat—the captain's seat. However, the pay was good, the flight schedules were good, and I was traveling to parts of the world that I would never have been able to see had I not been an international airline pilot with Pan Am.

From San Francisco, we flew mostly to the Pacific destinations such as Honolulu, Fiji, American Samoa, Hong Kong, Tokyo, Guam, Tahiti, and Sydney. A very exciting flight—although very tiring—was the Round the World flight. From San Francisco, we flew that flight in both directions: Flight One was the westbound flight and Flight Two was the eastbound flight.

The route of the eastbound flight was like this:
San Francisco,
London,
Beirut,
New Delhi,
Bangkok,
Hong Kong,
Tokyo, and
San Francisco.

These flights could be very tiring because we flew through so many time zones with no chance for our bodies to catch up until we arrived back home. Then it would take three days to get back to near normal. This was the result of throwing the circadian rhythm out of step, commonly known as "jet lag." After returning home, it would take several days for my body to get back to normal, and during some of that time, I would feel like a walking zombie. I could almost use the jet lag as my work calendar—by the time I was back to 100%, it would be time to return to work.

Jet lag naturally had an effect on pilots while flying on the line. The difference was, during the week that they were out flying, adrenaline came into play to help keep going. Also, knowing that they had a job to do, they kept focused on performing that job to the best of their ability, using greater than 100% effort, even though their body may only be functioning at 50-75%. It was important to be well rested before the next flight on each leg of the journey. When they got back home, the adrenaline wouldn't be flowing strongly, so they were able to relax, at which time they'd feel the full effects of jet lag. Or at least that was the way it affected me.

Pilots have tried every technique known to man to try to defeat jet lag, but none of it really works. Some even try to adjust their sleep routine to keep with the same time zone as their own home. It may trick the mind into thinking it helps, but the circadian rhythm is generated by an internal clock synchronized to light and dark cycles, so the sleep-changing technique doesn't work.

The body's rhythm is also known to be controlled mainly by the release of hormones. The internal clock for humans is located within the brain glands that release melatonin in response to information received from photoreceptors in the retina. During the night, melatonin secretion rises; during the day, it's inhibited. Even if light cues are absent, melatonin is still released in a cyclical manner.

Therefore, jet lag is virtually impossible to beat. You just learn to live and deal with it in your own way.

Like everyone else, I had a system that worked for me. Although it didn't relieve the jet lag symptoms, what was more important was that I was able to be rested when I needed to be rested. First and foremost, I made sure that I did my best to be rested for my next flight departure. What I did was go to sleep when I was tired. If I arrived at the hotel in London at 10:00 a.m. after flying all night, I would be tired and go to bed. I would often get up around 3:00 p.m. if I wanted to go shopping, go for a walk to exercise, or get tickets for a show that evening.

Sometimes the crew would get together for a cocktail, or go to dinner together. At any rate, I would usually go back to bed around 10-11:00 p.m. and set a wakeup call for 7:00 a.m. That way I would be rested for my flight the next day, even though I was still feeling the effects of jet lag.

Split the Check

Speaking of going out to dinner as a group, I have to say that some pilots are cheap. However, what I'm going to talk about here applies to just some of the skygods, or early captains.

At some layover cities, the times that we'd arrive and the lack of anything else to do made it conducive for the entire crew to get together for a couple of drinks and go to dinner. The flight attendants were not big eaters because they had to watch their weight, so they would order lighter meals.

The captain that I'll speak of now would order several cocktails for himself, an expensive appetizer, and the most expensive steak on the menu, then a big dessert followed by an after dinner liqueur. Just as an example, his meal might have cost $60 while the others might have cost only $20. When you go into a restaurant with a group of ten people, the waiters don't want to write separate checks. So can you guess what the captain would suggest? You got it right!

"Why don't we make it easy on the waiter and just split the bill ten ways. Here's my part."

No one liked that, but usually no one would say anything. Once a captain pulled that, then on subsequent flights no one who had been to dinner with him before would join him again. Fortunately, there were only a few pilots who were cheap enough to pull that stunt.

Visualization

I should talk a little more about visualization here because by this time I had read the book *Psycho-Cybernetics*, and had a basic understanding of programming the subconscious mind. I would use this to my advantage on the approach and landings, which would come at the end of a long day, at a time when I was tired, but really needed to be operating at 100%, or better.

Prior to leaving home, I would review the entire flight, in order to familiarize myself with the routes and approaches to the various destination and alternate airports for the routes we would be flying on that trip. Then, at the hotel, I would usually set my wakeup call in time to spend 30 minutes reviewing the departure route, en route charts, and the approach charts for the next destination and alternate airports. Then, on the airplane, about one hour prior to descent, I would review the approach and landing charts again, and begin to plan the approach and landing.

By reviewing these charts at home, and again at the hotel, I would become more familiar with the names of the navigation facilities, and find it easier to understand what the controller was saying if the destination was Delhi, Bangkok, Istanbul, or other foreign country where understanding their accent might be challenging.

On the airplane, prior to beginning the descent to our destination airport, I would again perform a thorough review of the approach procedure. After reviewing the approach charts, I would lay my head back against the headrest and close my eyes while the other pilot minded the airplane.

I would then visualize the approach and landing, starting from the top of descent. I would visualize every action throughout the approach. In my mind's eye, my hands would be handling the controls just as if I were actually flying the airplane. I would visualize turning to the final approach heading, adjusting the approach speed, and calling for lowering the landing gear and flaps at the proper time.

After intercepting the instrument landing system localizer, I would see myself on course, and then intercept the glide slope during the final approach. At the proper time, I would call for the landing gear, then full flaps, and then adjust to final approach speed. As we passed over the end of the runway at 100 feet, I would begin to flare the airplane by raising the nose to reduce the rate of descent, and reduce the throttle to decrease to landing speed, and then make a smooth touchdown.

Next, I would use reverse thrust and check that the speed brakes (spoilers) were deployed; then, at the proper speed, come out of reverse thrust and transition to the brakes.

This type of visualization was what I used throughout my flying career and was of exceptional value to me. It would make the actual approach and landing so much easier because I had studied the procedures three times prior to beginning the approach, and then I had visualized the entire approach and landing in my mind. My subconscious mind was then programmed to guide me through the approach. This type of visualization can be used for any purpose. It works. Try it.

My techniques, which I developed very early in my life without knowing what I was doing, are not unlike the techniques that Dr Maxwell Maltz teaches in his book, *Psycho-Cybernetics*, which I discovered in the early '70s, and continue to use today. After reading my book, I highly recommend picking up the latest edition of Dr. Maltz's book, *The New Psycho-Cybernetics*, published in 2001.

Chapter 13 –
Flying into Vietnam

It was always sad to see the long wooden boxes being loaded into the cargo hold of our airplanes during the stops in Vietnam. We knew what the boxes contained.

During the '60s and '70s, Pan Am flew many flights into Vietnam carrying cargo and passengers, in addition to the dreaded job of bringing back the bodies of our fallen soldiers. After Da Nang had fallen to the North Vietnamese in April 1975, and Saigon was under attack, being very heavily shelled, President Ford authorized the evacuation of Vietnamese orphans and Amerasian children of American servicemen and Vietnamese women, in an operation called Operation Babylift.

The purpose was meant to be a gesture to repatriate children who would be American citizens if they were recognized by their American fathers. The children were airlifted to various countries including Australia, Europe, America, and Canada, with volunteers including military nurses accompanying the children.

Many of these children suffered from malnutrition, and some were disabled. Many were adopted by volunteers who were on the flight, or by other American families. Pan Am participated in the Babylift flights during the final days of the Vietnam War in 1975, and also participated in the last flights that were taking government diplomats and our own Pan Am personnel out of Saigon.

On one of those last flights, a 747 only had a few diplomat

passengers aboard. It was going to leave Saigon with 176 empty seats. In their book *Flying, a Novel*, authors Paula Helfrich and Rebecca Sprecher, both former Pan Am flight attendants, relate the following story.

Zoe, a character in the book, asked Pan Am Ground Agent George Trinh if he had 176 refugees he would like to bring aboard. Mr. Trinh said he didn't have official authorization, but he did have a large group of military dependent spouses and sponsored individuals with military connections. He said these were mostly Doh Street bargirls and their Amerasian children, who had no status in Vietnam—and if they didn't leave with their children it would be very bad for both mother and child.

Zoe went upstairs to the 747 cockpit to speak with the captain, and asked if he would be willing to take un-manifested passengers on the flight, if they could get permission for them to land at Anderson AFB in Guam.

The captain asked, "Can I go to jail for doing this?"

Zoe replied, "Only if they catch us in Saigon."

"Then put them on and let's get the hell out of Saigon!"

As Paula and Rebecca demonstrate in their fictionalized account of this incident, there were times that the "book" had to be thrown out the window in order to get something worthwhile accomplished.

Difficult Approaches

Most of my flights into Vietnam were on the Boeing 707, taking soldiers to and from R&R destinations like Hong Kong, Manila, Bangkok, and Sydney. We were happy to be providing this service to our GIs, but flying in and out of Vietnam was not a lot of fun. We flew into three Vietnam bases: Cam Rahn Bay, Da Nang, and Saigon.

Cam Rahn Bay was relatively safe for us, but we would still make high, close-in steep approaches as a precaution against being hit by small arms fire on final approach. The thing that struck me about Cam Rahn Bay was the long curving coastline with beautiful white sand beaches. It's a deep water bay and one of the finest deep water shelters in Southeast Asia.

Da Nang, which is located farther to the north from Cam Rahn Bay, was the most scary and dangerous airport at which to land in Vietnam. The Viet Cong were always nearby, and they could launch rockets with pinpoint accuracy from the hills around the airport—and they did. We would come in very high on a downwind leg, then turn west toward land on base leg, and then make a very steep descent when we made our turn onto final approach. On take-off we climbed at a maximum angle and headed out over the sea as quickly as possible.

Saigon, now Ho Chi Minh City, was the safest airport at which to land until the North Vietnamese soldiers overtook the city, but that is also where we took some small arms rounds in the airplane's belly. It wasn't unusual to walk around the airplane after landing and find a small bullet hole. It would be patched with high speed tape and off we would go; it would get a permanent patch when the airplane got back to San Francisco. Stories circulated that some pilots would sit on phone books to protect their rear end from small arms fire, but they were just rumors. If a bullet got that far up into the airplane, I doubt that a phone book would protect the family jewels.

Many times, when we approached Saigon from the northeast, we would see "Puff the Magic Dragon," a modified AC-47 aircraft, raining down its continuous stream of fire from the Gatling machine guns mounted onboard. The guns were mounted on the left side of the airplane so the pilot would have the target to his left, and he would stay in a left bank circling around the target, with the guns firing. On our approach to Saigon, we could see the bright bullet tracers and follow their path to the ground. Each Gatling machine gun could fire from 2,000-6,000 rounds per minute, and could be controlled to a very tight range. It was sad to see the ravages of war happening just below us on those approaches.

French Onion Soup

Our stops in Saigon were brief, normally only one hour, but sometimes we would have a 2-3 hour stay. During those times we would head over to the airport restaurant to have the best French onion soup and French bread that I have ever tasted. The first time I ordered, I was surprised to discover some tiny black bug creatures baked into the bread. Apparently, they would get into the sacks of flour, and since there were too many to pick out, they just baked them in the bread. I suppose the high baking heat killed any germs, and I was told that the cooked bugs contained protein. Well, I loved the bread, but didn't think I needed any more protein, so I just picked the bugs out of the bread and kept eating.

The Souvenirs

In Da Nang, some of the female flight attendants would go visit the soldiers in flight operations. It had to be a very quick visit, because we wanted to get out of that airport as soon as the airplane was loaded and ready to go. I'm told that the walls in one of the rooms were decorated with a collection of Pan Am flight attendant panties. Apparently, the flight attendants would donate a pair for the collection. The word is that the panties were more valuable as a "collectors" item" if they were the ones the attendant was wearing when she went into visit operations. I was never in the operations office so I'm not able to confirm or deny that piece of information.

R&R

Each time we left Vietnam with a load of GIs going on R&R, they were all very awake, alert, energetic, and excited. They didn't appear to have come from a war zone. But I guess that's understandable; they were anxious to get away from battle and go to exotic locations for a week of partying.

During the early days, we all left the cockpit door open and told the soldiers they were welcome to come to the cockpit to look around and chat with us. Some of the young enlisted men were amazed because they had never seen the inside of a cockpit before, and some of the air force pilots were happy to come up and visit because they were hoping to be hired by an airline after their tour of duty. Most were young kids fighting for our country, not knowing why, and not knowing if they would ever go home again. Many of them didn't.

There were many humorous scenes during those flights, because all the pilots and flight attendants tried to make the flights fun for these brave guys. Helen Davey, a former Pan Am flight attendant, told a story in an article about a male purser who would joke with the guys as he gave the safety announcement.

During the briefing where the flight attendants point out the location of life rafts, the purser is supposed to say "forward," "center," and "aft." The flight attendants were programmed to point their hands toward forward, center and aft, in that order. Mr. Purser would turn it around and say, "You'll find the life rafts located in the aft, center and forward," but the flight attendants, by habit, would point to forward, center and aft—just the opposite of what he was saying.

Then Mr. Purser would say, "So you see guys, our young ladies are beautiful—but they don't know their forward from their aft!"

Of course, the soldiers would explode with laughter. Things like that broke the ice and helped those young guys relax for a while.

However, when they arrived at Bangkok or Hong Kong, to begin their R&R vacation, they wouldn't have to worry about relaxing. Just outside the Customs area would be a hundred young girls.

"Hi GI, you need a wife? I take good care of you."

So, for a week this "wife" would take good care of the young soldier. At the end of the week, she would be at the airport to see him off, and say, "Baby, I want to write you all time, so you leave me $100 for stamps, yes?"

After the soldiers got on the airplane, the "wives" would go over to the arrival area to greet the next batch of soldiers, where the story would be repeated:

"Hi GI, you need a wife? I take good care of you."

On the way back to Vietnam from their R&R week, the soldiers acted more like they were leaving a war zone instead of going to one. They were exhausted; the first thing they did was go to sleep. Some slept the entire way back to Vietnam without even eating.

To: All Pilots. From the Chief Pilot

The heading was ominous; however, it was only a letter informing us that a military colonel on one of the R&R flights complained that the pilot left the cockpit door open allowing soldiers to enter the cockpit, which was in violation of FAA regulations. Nothing more was said. We knew what he meant. He was saying he understood that "sometimes we have to throw out the book and do what we feel is best, and I'm not going to criticize any of you. I just need you to know that some colonel complained."

We also knew that we could be fined $1,000 if a complaint was filed with the FAA. So that colonel ended a generous practice of allowing our soldiers to have a peek inside the cockpit of an airplane, which may have been the only chance of that happening in their lifetime. Some of those who were denied the small pleasure of that once in a lifetime opportunity to see the inside of a cockpit in flight probably went home in the cargo compartment.

Chapter 14 –
Awarded a Training Captain Position

"Hello, Bill, this is Bill Frisbie. I'd like you to join the training department as a training captain. If you're interested, come to my office, and I'll explain the job."

"Would I? You're damn right I would!"

Becoming a training captain was never a goal of mine. I had never planned, nor did I ever expect, to be invited into the training department, but I was not going to pass up that opportunity.

Four times each year a pilot's career is placed on the line. The A check, the B check, the annual flight physical, and finally, the once a year route check with a check pilot on board. Fail any one of these, and the pilot's career may be over.

Every six months, an airline pilot must take a check ride in the simulator. The first is the A check. This is primarily a training session; there is no oral exam. However, if the pilot doesn't perform all the flight maneuvers and emergency functions safely, the pilot would have to take a couple of days off to study, and then repeat the failed maneuvers. It was not considered a failed check, just extra training. However, if after the study and the repeat training ride, they pilot still could not perform the maneuvers safely, a conversation with the Manager of Flight Training would be required. The next session then becomes a check ride which the pilot must pass, after one more training session prior to the check ride.

The next six-month check is the B check; this is all check ride—no training. It begins with a one-hour oral exam, then a discussion of the maneuvers to be performed in the simulator, and then into the simulator for the check ride. There would be a first officer and a captain getting the check ride at the same time. The captain would be checked first, taking two hours, followed by a thirty-minute break, and then the first officer would get his turn.

During the check ride, the pilot not being checked must perform the support job for the pilot being checked, just as he would on the line, and is actually being checked for how well he supports the other pilot.

Several weeks prior to my scheduled check ride, I would begin studying all of the normal, alternate, and emergency procedures; there were so many procedures that we didn't use on the line every day, so we needed to review them often. Then I would review all of the instrument approaches that we would be expected to fly, and review all of the engine fire, engine failure, and other emergency procedures.

Next, I would put my visualization techniques to work. I would close my eyes and picture myself in the simulator cockpit flying the airplane through every one of the approaches and emergency procedures. I would visualize myself performing every operation just as if I were in the actual airplane cockpit. As I've said before, this is not a new technique—basketball players, golf players, and other major sport players use visualization in their practice. That's because visualization is highly successful as a practice technique.

The B Check

On one particular occasion, the training captain giving me the B check ride was Captain Bill Frisbie, who later became the Manager of Flight Training, and still later was promoted to San Francisco

Chief Pilot. Captain Frisbie was a perfect candidate for the chief pilot job because he was a "pilot's pilot." By that, I mean one who is highly skilled and knowledgeable, yet modest about his skills, and treats everyone else with respect. That was Captain Bill Frisbie.

As usual, I had prepared well for the check ride because I never wanted to have a failed check ride on my record. I was still a 707 first officer, and the captain and flight engineer, who were also getting their check ride, were both very sharp. Consequently, the check ride went smoothly, and we all went about our normal schedules.

It was several months later, after Captain Frisbie became Manager of the Flight Training department, that he made the phone call to me. There was a pay raise involved and my new title was "Training Captain."

I should explain that all first officers with Pan Am had the Boeing 707 Type Rating issued by the FAA. That means we were qualified to fly as captain. It was only due to the lack of seniority in the company that we flew as first officer. The reason we had to get the Type Rating was that on long flights, where we had a relief pilot, there always had to be a pilot in the seat who was qualified to be pilot in command (captain). All of the Pan Am first officers had the Type Rating for the airplane they flew, so as far as the FAA was concerned, we were captains. Therefore, on long flights, Pan Am was getting the extra captain, which was required by the FAA, for the price of a first officer. That was no problem, it was pure economics, and we understood. Not that we liked it, but we did understand.

A training captain would be chosen from the first officer ranks because it was cheaper to pay a first officer the extra training captain pay than it would be to pay a captain his captain pay. At the risk of confusing matters further, a "training captain" is different from a "check captain." A check captain is someone who observes the in-flight operation of the crew—remember that once a year route check? That check captain was a Pan Am captain who would normally fly the line as a captain, not a first officer.

The training captain's job is to conduct the A and B check rides in the simulator, and also conduct training in the airplane when necessary. The training captain must be qualified to fly from either the left or right seat. There is a big difference in flying from the two seats because the visual perception when lining up with the runway is a lot different; the control wheel and throttles are operated with different hands in the different seats. Because of that, it takes a little time to adjust to flying from the other seat. Training captains had to be able to fly from either seat at any time, and since we were doing this four times a week, we could automatically adjust to either seat without thinking.

The training captain job had some perks: I only worked four days a week; I was home every night; it was a raise in pay; and by instructing, I became much more proficient, and an even better pilot. Also, when an opportunity arose to fly a volunteer charity mission, the training captains were able to do that.

On February 4, 1976, there were several earthquakes with magnitudes up to 7.5 near Guatemala City that killed twenty-three thousand people, leaving one million, five hundred thousand people homeless. Captain Frisbie, a flight engineer and I flew a volunteer flight (that means no pay) to Guatemala to deliver supplies. Pan Am donated the aircraft, while others donated the supplies we delivered. Pan Am was always there to help when needed.

Skygods

While I was still a 707 training captain in the training department, the Boeing 747s came into service. In San Francisco, we had simulators for both the 707 and the 747, so we would regularly see the

747 pilots come into the training department. Because the 747 was so new, and because it was a larger airplane with higher pay, it was highly desirable to check out on the 747. Consequently, the opportunity was only available to the most senior pilots. Some of the 747 captains at that time were very close to retirement, and had flown the Boeing Stratocruiser, which had been superseded in the early '60s. Some had even been on the Clipper Flying Boats, which had ceased production in 1941.

Robert Gandt, a Pan Am pilot and well respected aviation author, referred to these earlier pilots as "skygods," and wrote a book titled *Skygods: The Fall of Pan Am,* an excellent book with a lot of detail on some of the accidents and incidents leading to the demise of Pan Am.

In a way, some of those early pilots were demigods who seemed to think of their word as the gospel. First officers were not allowed to tell these skygods anything, no matter how wrong the captains were. This dictatorial leadership style led to a series of accidents in the 1970s that resulted in a dramatic change in the Pan Am training and operation procedures, and the creation of the "crew concept" method of cockpit leadership that is in use by most airlines today.

The crew concept leadership style requires all crew members to cross check everything, and point out any potential problem to the captain. Time permitting, the captain should solicit input from all crew members and weigh all available information before making a decision. The captain still makes the final decision. Throughout this book, you have seen, and will see, more examples of the crew concept of leadership in operation. We were teaching crew concept leadership when I was in the training department. In fact, it's the concept that I've always operated under, even while I was with Zantop, prior to joining Pan Am. It was only when I flew with some of the Pan Am skygods that I was exposed to the dictatorial method of cockpit leadership.

But back to the sought-after 747: Those who were in training to be 747 pilots developed a different walk; a swagger of sorts. When a pilot walked down the hall of the training building, we could immediately tell by the swagger that he was a 747 pilot (trainee).

One of the pilots, who was in training to be a 747 captain, wrote that since the 747 was a "Super Airplane," that the 747 captains should be designated as "Super Captains," and they should be set apart from the other pilots by having different uniforms. Pan Am had black uniforms with white hats. This pilot suggested that the 747 "Super Captains" should have white uniforms with white hats.

The other pilots couldn't believe what this pilot was suggesting, but he had gone so far as to put it in writing as a suggestion to the company. The suggestion was never taken up, and 747 pilots kept the same classic Pan Am uniform as everyone else. The ironic part of this story is that this particular captain failed in his attempt to check out on the 747. He never became a "Super Captain." He was relegated to flying as a lowly, regular 707 captain for the rest of his career.

Chapter 15 – Checked Out on the Boeing 747

Landing the 747 was unlike any other airplane I had ever flown. It was like landing a four-story building; the pilot seat in the cockpit was thirty feet off the ground. When the airplane is flared for landing, with the nose up, the main wheels touch the ground first, and at that moment, the pilot seat is about forty feet off the ground. It took a while in the simulator to get used to the height, in order to know where the main wheels would be at forty feet above them on touchdown, but as soon I became accustomed to the size of the aircraft, I always knew when the wheels were about to touch down. It was just a matter of time and practice.

Another aspect of that height is the speed perception. From inside the cockpit looking out, it appears that the airplane is taxiing about five miles an hour, when it's actually going 25-30 mph. From the ground looking up at a 747 climbing out, or on an approach to landing, the airplane appears to be moving very slowly compared to the smaller airplanes like the 727, but the 747 is actually going faster. It's the size—twice as big as a 707—that makes it appear to be going slower.

When my seniority allowed me to check out as first officer on the 747, I left the training captain position because it was a step closer to my goal of flying the line as captain. The 747 first officer pay was also higher.

Photo by RobertS/BigStockPhoto

747 Training

During ground training for the 747, I was paired with Captain John Bell. John was upgrading from 707 captain to 747 captain, while I was making the same jump as first officer. However, I still had to take the same check ride as the captain, because we both had to get the FAA 747 Type Rating.

Competition

John was extremely sharp, and a fast learner. So, being competitive, I had to make sure that I kept up with him. Part of the teaching method was to assign a home study lesson, and then cover that material the next day in class. The instructor would begin by asking questions about each system we were to have studied the night before. If a pilot hadn't studied, it would become obvious immediately. Using this technique helped us prepare for the one-hour oral exam we would have when we were ready to take our check ride for the 747 Type Rating.

I knew John was sharp because, while I was a 707 training captain, I had given John a B check—which he passed with flying colors. Since I had seen John in action, I knew his capabilities, and became determined to not let him get ahead of me. I probably kept a little pressure on John also, because all through the training we were both highly prepared for the day's lesson. As I've stated before, I always programmed my mind, and worked hard to be prepared to pass all my check rides; I was determined to never fail. However, in this training I had to set my goal a little higher, and that was to make sure I kept up with John Bell.

The sequence was to go through the ground school first, using a cockpit mockup to learn all the systems and switches and the Normal, Alternate and Emergency check lists. After completing that training, we would go into the simulator to perform the actual maneuvers. After the simulator training, we would be ready for our Type Rating check ride, which would consist of a one-hour oral exam, followed by a four-hour simulator check, with the captain being checked the first two hours and the first officer being checked the second two hours.

The entire process, from class on day one, to taking our check ride, took about seven weeks—a far cry from the six months that it took to check out as flight engineer back in 1966. During this training, it was great fun being paired with John, who was such an outstanding pilot. We both passed the oral and check ride with flying colors.

Skygods Revisited

Prior to the 747, the cabin and flight crew were a more harmonized group. The 707 pilots were not isolated on an upper deck, and they were more interested in having a good working relationship with the cabin crew. The 707 pilots provided the flight attendants all the support they needed, and in turn they treated us well.

The company provided crew meals, which were not as appetizing as eating in the First Class section, but by treating the flight attendants well they would give us any of the first class meals that were left over, after they had their choice, of course.

When going through Customs in some foreign countries, it was not unusual for some of the Customs agents to try to intimidate the female flight attendants; usually they just wanted the flight attendants to give them decks of Pan Am playing cards and other items from the airplane. So we pilots would be in the back of the line, behind the ladies, so we could see what was going on and say something if we felt a Customs agent was getting out of line.

The 747 skygods took a different tack, which drastically changed the working relationship between the flight and cabin crews for years. These captains began to lobby Pan Am to put them in separate luxury hotels. Some of them felt they were too good to stay with the rest of the crew. One made the statement to me that since familiarity breeds contempt, the 747 captains deserve to be housed in different quarters from the rest of the staff. Well, he was partly right. It only took a brief conversation to breed contempt for this captain. They also wanted separate transportation to and from the airport and hotel. There were 14 flight attendants and these skygods didn't want to wait for them to get through Customs.

The company gave the 747 flight crew separate transportation, which was a bad move, in my opinion. But they didn't get separate hotels. Since they now had separate transportation, the 747 captains would rush to the front of the Customs line and get in their crew bus and leave. They would be at their hotel before the flight attendants got through Customs.

I was appalled at the lack of respect these skygods displayed towards their cabin crew; so, each time we started to go through Customs, I would tell the captain that it would take me longer to get through and that he should go ahead without me. Then I would get in the back of the line so I could support the flight attendants if they were harassed by the Customs personnel.

Team Concept

An airline crew should function as a team because, in the event of an emergency, they must all work together to get through the emergency situation safely. If there is friction and stress operating below the surface between the crew members, safety can be compromised. Eventually all of the skygods were retired, and a new younger breed moved into their seats. This new generation recognized the need to develop more of a team concept of leadership, and thus began the long road to healing the wounds created by the skygods.

I must be quick to state that most of these skygod types were excellent aviators, and were instrumental in pioneering Pan Am's routes, helping to make Pan Am the great airline it was. It's just unfortunate that, in the end, a few of their attitudes caused so much damage.

Not only did their attitudes create friction between the cabin and cockpit crews, the skygod leadership concept during those days did not allow or encourage teamwork, or the use of the "crew concept" of flying the airplane. Consequently, the lack of the crew concept was determined to be the cause of some of the accidents Pan Am experienced during the 1970s.

Chapter 16 – Flying without Fear of Terrorism

It was eleven o'clock in the morning, and I was on a three-hour layover in Los Angeles. My cousin John and his family had just arrived so I could give them a tour of the Pan Am 707. They didn't have to go through a security line, they just walked into the terminal and down to the gate where my airplane was parked. How did that happen? Well, let me explain.

The year was 1968. On the day before, I had telephoned John to invite him and his family to come to the airport and visit for a while, because my flight was going to be on the ground there for two hours.

It was the first time any of them had been inside a jet airplane, and John's kids were in awe of this big jet. What a treat! The airplane had already been cleaned in preparation for the next flight, and I was the only crew member aboard at this time; the rest of the crew had gone to the restaurant to have a snack. We had the airplane all to ourselves for about half an hour.

During the 1960s, John or anyone else could go directly to the boarding gate. There were no security lines, no searches, and no body-scanners. No one went through your luggage, messing up your neatly folded clothes. You didn't have to get half undressed and go barefoot through a metal detector, then hobble over to pick up your belongings at the end of the conveyer to get dressed again, hoping your pants didn't fall down because you had had to remove your belt.

You didn't have to walk into an x-ray machine, hold up your hands and have them snap a picture that makes your clothes invisible, but shows your nude body for someone to steal and place on the internet. In fact, there was no internet. Al Gore hadn't invented it yet!

You just casually walked down to the gate like you would walk into any shopping mall. How cool is that? If you were meeting people who were arriving on a flight, you went straight to the gate and greeted them when they got off the airplane. If you had a limo waiting, the driver would have his sign in the air as you walked off the airplane.

Once the acts of terrorism began, airline flying became a vastly different world. Now it is a world of fear and distrust. Who is that passenger that looks different from me? Is he a terrorist? Will he blow up the airplane? We didn't have to worry about that during the "good ole days." Today there are too many strange things going on, and we're constantly on alert.

It was a pleasure to visit with John and his family during that short half hour, but unfortunately, it turned out to be the last time I would see John. Not long after they visited me at the airport, John was killed in a motorcycle accident; his family relocated to Tennessee, and I lost contact with them. Many years later, during a visit to my parents in Tennessee, I ran into John's son, who reminded me of his visit to the Pan Am jet cockpit back in 1968. He said he still remembered that visit to the 707. "What a thrill it was," he said, "being able to sit in the captain's seat, and take away some decks of Pan Am playing cards and Jr. Pilot wings as souvenirs."

Pan Am Playing cards? Jr. Pilot wings? What are those, you ask? Well, today they're "collector's items," but unfortunately, they're something you'll probably never see on an airline again. The good ole days of flying in luxury and feeling comfortable and secure are long gone.

Chapter 17 –
That Can't Be My First Officer!

It was a hot, humid, August night, and a line of towering thunderstorms was running along the east coast from Boston to Carolina. The dark night was continuously lit up by the bright flashes of thunderbolts dancing between the clouds and shooting directly down to the ground; the thunder was deafening. This was the type of night when I would wish I was at home curled up by the fireplace with my wife. It was going to be an interesting departure from Washington D.C. to London that evening—and I didn't realize just how interesting it was going to be.

I had been sent to D.C. the day before to take this flight. The first officer was deadheading (traveling on duty, but as a passenger) from New York to arrive just in time for the flight. So, I never met the first officer until I reported to Flight Operations at 7:00 p.m. When I arrived at operations, I approached the dispatcher, who pointed across the room and said the first officer already had the paperwork over at a work table. I turned around, and couldn't believe what I was seeing.

"You've got to be kidding me; is this practical joke or something? That can't be my first officer!"

Across the room, standing at the work table, was a living replica of a Barbie doll; she was every bit of five feet tall, with long blond hair halfway down her back. That was my first officer? Would her feet reach the rudder pedals? Could she see out the window without sitting on a phone book? I would have to fly around all these thunderstorms through the busiest air corridor in the world—over Washington, Baltimore, Philadelphia, New York, and Boston—with a Barbie doll in the right seat. And I'd probably have to watch my language too.

Lord, was it something I said?

In 1986, Pan Am purchased a commuter airline from Ransome Airlines and named it Pan Am Express. Among the pilots they hired were several women, most of whom had had a distinguished military career prior to joining Pan Am Express. While flying with Pan Am Express, they increased their skills by flying through the difficult and challenging airports and icy weather conditions in the northeastern states. As openings for pilots at Pan Am occurred, Pan Am hired pilots from Pan Am Express first. I had flown with a couple of the male pilots that had been hired from Pan Am Express and found them to be excellent pilots, but I had never met any of the female pilots.

Our jet airplanes were much faster on final approach than these pilots were accustomed to on their de Havilland Canada Dash 7 airplanes, so for a while they were a little behind the airplane on final approach, but when they got near the ground they were caught up and would make enviable landings. We had a lot of respect for the skills and positive attitudes of these younger pilots.

Unfortunately, I don't remember the name of this lady, so I'm going to refer to her as Barbie, because of her long blond hair. She was a lovely lady and an expert pilot, so if she ever reads this, I hope she understands that the reference to her as Barbie is with the utmost respect.

I walked over to the work area feeling a bit uncomfortable. Although I knew that this lady was highly qualified and had the skills to be where she was, I still had to get over the fact that my mind was programmed to see a male first officer in that seat, not a five-foot-short, blonde female. This was going to be my first time with a female pilot, and I had to quickly develop a new mindset.

"Hello, I'm Bill Travis, and I think we're going to London together."

"Hello Skipper, I'm Barbie and I'm glad to meet you. I've checked the paperwork, drawn the route on the chart for us, and here are the weather reports. It looks like we'll have thunderstorms all the way until we pass the Boston area where it should be clear sailing the rest of the way. London is forecast to be clear with unlimited visibility for our arrival."

"Good job, Barbie, thank you, I'll get my work done, and we can head out to the airplane. Do you have a raincoat to use for your airplane walk around"?

"Yes, sir, I'm all prepared; I even have my rubbers."

So far, so good, and she had a sense of humor. Each time a captain flies with a new first officer (FO), there is a learning curve to see how helpful the FO is going to be, their personality, and how much they can rely on him, or in this case, her. Sometimes, the FO may be new enough on the airplane that the captain would have to keep a close eye on them to catch any mistakes they may make because of it being a new aircraft for them.

Also, some FOs may not be assertive enough to take the initiative, and the captain would have to push them a little. With that type, the captain has to be ever vigilant. For the really sharp assertive FOs, the captain can concentrate more on his own duties knowing that the FO will be doing his or her job well. The captain doesn't have to be constantly watching the sharp FO to make sure things are done right. He knows that the FO will do a good job.

So far, Barbie had been assertive, prepared, and had done a thorough job of checking the flight plan, so I was beginning to relax. But we were still on the ground; she was still a five-foot-short blonde—young enough to be my daughter—appearing to need a booster seat to see the instrument panel,- and that night we had a line of towering thunderstorms to circumnavigate in the busiest flight corridor in the world. As my country cousin Clarence would say, "We'll be busier than a rooster in a hen house."

Control Checks

During pre-flight checks, part of the routine is to see that the flight controls move free and easy. The rudder pedals are pushed to the far right and then to the far left. On top of the yoke is the wheel that controls the ailerons. Turn left to bank left; turn right to bank right. The aileron is turned fully to the left, and then fully to the right to check that they are free to move full throw.

The yoke is the large column that pivots from the cockpit floor, about four inches in diameter, which controls the elevator. Pull back and the airplane goes up; push forward and the airplane goes down. To check the elevator movement, the yoke is pushed full forward, and then full back. There is a large split in the center of the pilot seats to allow the yoke to come back all the way; the split ends right at the pilot's crotch. If the captain is seated a little forward, and the other pilot who is checking the controls doesn't give any warning when the yoke is pulled back, the captain could be in for some excruciating pain.

Barbie was doing the control checks; she checked the rudders, then the ailerons, and next was the yoke. After pushing the yoke forward, she said, "Okay, Skipper, watch your jewels, the yoke is coming back."

"Thanks for the warning, Barbie; I've been hit before."

Departure

After completing our pre-flight checks, I proceeded to give the departure briefing. "Barbie, on this departure we'll be taking off on runway 19L with a right turn out climbing to 4,000 feet, then, as per the departure route, until intercepting airway J75. If we have an emergency that requires an immediate return to land, we're not going to dump fuel with these thunderstorms around; instead, we'll plan on an overweight landing on runway 19C because it will be closer than 19L and is the same length. In that event, be prepared to double check everything I do, and make sure I'm doing it right. Call out anything you see me doing wrong."

"Yes, sir, Skipper, you got it, but we're not going to have an emergency. I've got some shopping to do at Harrods in London."

So far she was batting 1,000. She did all of her paperwork properly, was prepared to do the walk around in the rain with rain coat and rubbers, helped me protect the family jewels, and then I learned that she was a lady who visualizes, sets goals, and thinks positively. And, by the way, she could reach the rudder pedals; the seat adjusted up so she looked taller when seated. While taxiing out, she handled the communications and setting up of all our radio and radar equipment efficiently, so I was feeling more and more relaxed.

"Clipper 54, cleared for take-off runway 19L, right turn out heading 270, climb to 4,000 feet. After take-off contact departure 134.4."

Barbie repeated the clearance and we began the take-off roll. After we were airborne, Barbie changed the radio frequency to departure control.

"Dulles departure, this is Clipper 54, climbing to 4,000."

"Roger Clipper 54, Dulles departure, continue climb to 6,000, turn right to heading 350."

"Clipper 54 climbing to 6,000. There's a heavy cell at that heading. Give us another heading please."

"Do you want to go right or left of the cell?"

"To the left."

"Clipper 54, stop your heading at 300. Advise when clear."

"Turning to heading 300, thank you."

Due to the close proximity of the thunderstorms in the fast moving cold front weather system, the flight was bumpy all the way to Boston.

Barbie looked at me, smiling, and said, "Damn, you're a rough driver, Skipper; can't you fly any smoother than this?"

Now she'd won my confidence completely. I knew I was in good hands. This lady was a pilot's pilot. She had been completely on top of every situation, and far ahead of the aircraft. From the time we started to taxi, all the way through the thunderstorms in the low level, extremely busy area, all I had to do was fly the airplane while she took care of everything else. That's exactly the way it should be. Barbie was a highly polished professional.

I knew that all the pilots who came from Pan Am Express were sharp pilots, and I had no doubt that Barbie would be no exception. It was just that it was new to me, having a female first officer, and a very short female at that, when I was accustomed to having male first officers as tall, or taller, than I am.

I've always respected women's right to have any job a male could have, and I respected this female pilot's right to be in her position. She earned that right the same as I did. Dee and I have three daughters, and we would never want them to be held back from a male-dominated profession. I had the opportunity to fly with two more female pilots before I retired, and I had the utmost respect for all of them.

After we got out of the northeast corridor, and were on our ocean route, we weren't too busy and had time to have a conversation.

Barbie told me she had flown military jets; then she got married to a civilian and decided to get out of the military and take a job with Pan Am Express. Her husband worked in the New York area where she was based.

She went on to say that since Pan Am had so many women pilots now, the company needed to make some changes. She said the first change they needed to make—and the female pilots are drafting a letter to the CEO demanding this—was the name of the cockpit.

I started thinking, for years the flight deck has been called the cockpit, and no one had ever questioned it. Now these female pilots—whom I respected up to this point—want to change the name of the flight deck from cockpit to something else?

She continued on to say that the name cockpit is a sexist name, and to prove it she asked, "What would you call a pit full of snakes? A snake pit, right?"

She continued, saying, "Okay, so since us women are here now, we feel the name should be changed to the Box Office!"

Now I was ROFLMAO. I had been had. Well, at least I knew I didn't have to be worried about my language.

Chapter 18 –
The Celebrity Passengers

Marlon Brando

Marlon Brando was a frequent flyer on our Pan Am flights; it wasn't unusual to see him on one of our Tahiti flights because he spent much of his time there during his breaks from filming. In 1965, after filming *Mutiny on the Bounty*, he purchased a 99-year lease for the island of Tetiaroa, which is located about 35 miles to the north of Tahiti. Tetiaroa is an atoll, an island of coral surrounding a lagoon, consisting of 12 small islands.

Mr. Brando was on several of the Pan Am flights I piloted and while I never had a conversation with him, he would always stop by the cockpit to say hello when he came onboard, and goodbye when he disembarked. The flight attendants were very excited any time he was on board, and after he made the movie, *The Godfather*, they would always remark that they were going to make him an offer he couldn't refuse. I never found out whether he refused or accepted any of the offers.

When we flew from Tahiti to Honolulu, the route would take us due north, just to the west of Tetiaroa. If Mr. Brando was onboard, as we approached the island we would make an announcement stating that we would be passing the Tetiaroa atoll, which would be visible on the right side of the aircraft. Then we would make a slight bank so he could get a good view of the island. As a courtesy, to respect his privacy, we would never mention his name as we pointed out the island.

The last time I recall seeing Marlon Brando onboard, it was a sad occasion. We had taken him on our Pan Am flight from Tahiti to Honolulu, and from there he would change to a flight going to Los Angeles. Upon arriving at the gate in Honolulu, the airport manager met Mr. Brando and informed him that his lifelong friend, Wally Cox, had died. Mr. Brando was obviously distraught over this news, and continued on to Los Angeles where he helped with the funeral plans for Mr. Cox. It has been reported that Marlon Brando kept possession of Wally Cox's ashes; then, after Mr. Brando died, in 2004, his ashes were scattered along with Wally Cox's in Death Valley and Tahiti.

Sometime after Mr. Brando's death, a company purchased Tetiaroa from the Marlon Brando estate and started constructing a luxury eco-resort with completion planned for 2013. This resort was Brando's vision, so they named the hotel "The Brando." When completed, it will have 35 deluxe villas and offer various activities including archaeological tours of royal Tahitian sites.

Greenland

Being able to see Greenland as we passed overhead was a once in a lifetime opportunity for most of our passengers because on most days it was too cloudy to see anything. Fortunately, many of my Pan Am flights from London to New York were on days when Greenland was visible. Since I knew it was such a beautiful sight that most passengers would only have one chance to experience, I always told my passengers to expect that if Greenland was visible I would wake them up so they could enjoy the view.

The only complaints I received about waking the passengers

were from the flight attendants. That was understandable because once the passengers were asleep, the flight attendants could take their rest breaks. After the passengers were awakened to see Greenland, they would keep the flight attendants busy with drink requests, which would spoil their rest schedule. However, even though it interrupted their rest, our Pan Am flight attendants were very understanding, and they were also able to enjoy the view.

The best seat in the house for this view was in the cockpit. We had a 180 degree panoramic view; to say it was spectacular would be an understatement. On one flight, my wife was traveling with me, and we snuck her into the cockpit so she could enjoy this spectacular view from the next-to-the-best seat in the house, which is the jump seat directly behind the captain. Because I always maintained a good working relationship with the flight attendants, they didn't mind. They also, on occasion, got to enjoy the view from the cockpit.

Greenland Photo by Paxal/BigStockPhoto.com

Polar Bears

As we approached Greenland, I would lower the wing on the right side, and then on the left side, so the passengers on both sides of the airplane, and in the center seats, could get a better view of the magnificent glaciers. I would then make my usual announcement:

"If you look closely, down on the left side, you may see a polar bear and her cubs."

That was always fun because people would actually look for them. Of course, after a few minutes they would realize I was joking with them, so they would have a laugh at that.

My wife later said, "You lied. You can't see white polar bears from up here!"

Gotcha

As the passengers disembarked at our destination, it was customary for the captain to stand at the cockpit door to say goodbye and thank them for flying with Pan Am. Most of the passengers, as they were leaving, would comment about how much seeing Greenland meant to them. Occasionally, someone would hand me a note, expressing in writing what the experience meant to them. But on one particular day, a gentleman with a gruff voice came up to me, appearing to be a bit angry and said,

"I was sleeping very soundly up until some guy got on the microphone, woke me from my sound sleep, and started talking about Greenland and polar bears; was that you, Captain?"

I said, "Yes, sir, and I apologize for disturbing you, but most people want to be awakened for that view because they may never see it again."

His demeanor changed, and he said, adding a sly grin,

"Well, Captain, I just want to thank you for waking me. It was the most beautiful sight I have ever seen in my life, and I would not have wanted to miss it."

As he turned to walk away, he said, "But I didn't see any damn polar bears!"

His face was familiar, but at the moment I couldn't put a name to the face. I was still stunned by the way he got in my face, complaining, although he was actually happy. So I asked the flight attendant who he was, and she said, "Oh, that's Nick Nolte."

Prince Philip, Duke of Edinburgh

We were getting ready to taxi out at Tokyo's Narita airport, on our way to San Francisco, when the first class purser came upstairs to the cockpit of the 747. She told us that Prince Philip, Queen Elizabeth's consort (husband), was on board, and that his valet would like to hang the prince's garment bag in the cockpit. We had a large storage area, so that was fine with us.

We knew Prince Philip was a pilot, so we told the purser to extend our invitation for him to join us in the cockpit for take-off. This was against FAA regulations, but what the hell, sometimes you just have to throw the book out the window. This was the husband of the Queen of England—the Duke of Edinburgh—and he was a pilot, so we were willing to break the rules for the Royal Family.

The prince accepted our invitation, came into the cockpit, and sat in the jump seat behind the captain. The pilots had not been advised in advance that Prince Philip would be aboard, but fortunately, we did know how to address him, otherwise we may have been a little embarrassed. When you first speak with a prince, you address him as "Your Royal Highness." Thereafter, you use "Sir," unless he indicates that you may be casual.

When we began taxiing, we encountered a problem with the fuel tank indicators. The flight engineer knew we were fueled properly because he had checked the fuel closely; however, the gauges were now showing some unbalanced fuel tanks, and that issue had to be resolved before we could take off. Prince Philip was having a normal conversation with us, just as if he were another Pan Am pilot, and he got involved with the flight engineer, trying to help him find the solution to the problem. Fortunately, the flight engineer, with Prince Philip's able assistance, solved the problem prior to us reaching the take-off point, so we didn't have to delay the departure.

During the conversation, Prince Philip told us that, during his tour, he would be making several stops around the U.S. to give speeches. He was scheduled to speak in San Francisco, stay the night, and then go to Los Angeles the following day. After we leveled off at cruise altitude, and had a casual chat with the prince for a few minutes, he went back downstairs; but before he left, we invited him to come back up for the San Francisco landing.

Prior to beginning the descent into San Francisco, the prince's valet came to retrieve his garment bag so he could change into a fresh suit before disembarking, and after changing clothes, he came back up for the descent and landing. Fortunately, it was a beautiful, clear day in San Francisco, and we had the perfect approach in store for our royal guest.

Bay Approach

The Bay approach to the San Francisco airport provided a spectacular, even breathtaking view of this beautiful area. The approach began over the ocean, proceeded down the inlet, over the Golden Gate Bridge, then over the Bay, and crossed over Alcatraz Island before turning southeast and crossing over the Bay Bridge. Throughout this time, the magnificent city of San Francisco was on the right side of the airplane, and on the left side we could see Alameda, Oakland, and in the distance, Mt. Diablo.

After passing over the Bay Bridge, we proceeded southeast toward the San Mateo Bridge, but prior to reaching the bridge itself, we began a right turn onto base leg. Then we made a gradual turn onto the final approach heading, staying a little high, so as to not create noise over Foster City, which was built during the early 1960s on engineered landfill in the marshlands of San Francisco Bay, right under the approach to the San Francisco Airport.

After the Foster City residents moved in, they began to complain about the airport noise, so the airport authority and airlines had to develop noise restriction procedures, which made the approaches more difficult. It wasn't like they didn't know there was an international airport only five miles away, and yet they bought homes directly under the final approach path!

On that approach, we gave the Duke of Edinburgh a guided, scenic, aerial tour of the San Francisco Bay area fit for a prince.

Steve McQueen

We brought Steve McQueen, his wife, and makeup man back from Hong Kong after he finished filming *Sand Pebbles* in 1966, shortly after I had started flying the line as a flight engineer. We had heard he was a man of few words, and that turned out to be the case. He said hello to all the flight attendants, then said he was going to sleep and to please not disturb him. He didn't want to have dinner. Later we learned that he had not felt well because he had an abscessed molar, and had not wanted to see a dentist until he returned to California.

Laurence Harvey

We were on our way from London to Los Angeles, and several movie stars were on board, including Hugh O'Brien, who played Wyatt Earp on the TV show, and Laurence Harvey, who played Col. William B Travis in *The Alamo*.

O'Brien and Harvey had brought their own wine and caviar onboard with them. Apparently the wine and caviar Pan Am served was not good enough for them. But Pan Am was there to please, and if people wanted to bring their own wine, that was okay. They just had to give it to the flight attendants and have it served to them.

I was a 707 flight engineer at the time, and was doing my outside pre-flight inspection when O'Brien and Harvey walked across the tarmac to the airplane. I noticed that Harvey's walk was not exactly as I had seen him walk in the movies. Later, during the flight, the purser came to the cockpit and said, "That Laurence Harvey swishes up and down the aisle more than I do, and he stays in the bathroom longer than Mia Farrow"—who apparently was known to go into the toilet and stay for up to half an hour. What does one do in an airplane toilet for a half hour?

I had seen Laurence Harvey in several films, including the Alamo, which was filmed in 1960, and had remembered him from that film because of my second cousin relationship to Colonel Travis, the character he portrayed. On film, Harvey had a very masculine voice, as well as a masculine walk, but off screen, on that airplane, he was a very different person, and it surprised me to see that transformation.

In fact, it was the movie portrayals that were the transformation, because in real life, on that airplane, he appeared and acted in a stereotypically gay fashion; he walked with a swish, far from a masculine walk, and spoke very much like an openly gay person. During those years, most of the gay actors didn't come out because their career could be damaged. Was he gay? I don't know. I only know how he acted on the airplane.

During my break, I was in the front 707 lounge talking with another passenger, and Harvey came up to chat. His voice caught me by surprise because it was nothing like his on-screen voice. He told us about the Rolls Royce he had recently purchased. Then he mentioned that he made a lot of money, lived in a big house (the one that Ryan Seacrest bought from Ellen DeGeneres in 2012 for thirty-seven million dollars), and lived the movie star life to the fullest. It was interesting to hear the brief synopsis of his luxurious movie star life.

Senator Dianne Feinstein

Senator Feinstein and her husband were on our 747 flight from San Francisco to London one evening. During that time, she was the popular mayor of San Francisco. On this particular flight, I took my wife with me because we had a two-day layover in London before returning to San Francisco. Once our children were grown, I took her with me on trips that would interest her as often as I could. On this flight, she was in the seat in front of Mayor Feinstein, and had the opportunity to have a brief conversation with her, which was a memorable moment for Dee because Mayor Feinstein was someone she admired.

At some point during my flights, I would try to go through the cabin and say hello to some of the passengers, and I particularly wanted to say hello to Mayor Feinstein. It was about an hour and a half before arrival time, dawn was breaking, and people were waking up and beginning to move around. Often, people would change into more comfortable clothes after they were settled in for a long flight, and Mayor Feinstein had done just that.

At the moment I arrived by her seat to say hello, she had her blanket raised up, covering herself while changing back into her skirt. It was a rather embarrassing moment for her, and for me, but she took it in stride, and her husband joked with her saying, "I told you to go to the lavatory to change but you wouldn't listen."

We all had a laugh, and chatted for a couple of minutes. Then I went back upstairs to the cockpit.

Robert Ashley: Is That You, Bill?

I may have chosen the aviation route for my career—and with my visualization, goal setting and hard work, I had a very good 35 years traveling that route—but music was still my other love, and I had fond memories of all the members of the 4th Armored Division Band who became my best friends and, in so many ways, my mentors.

While I was flying as a Pan Am captain on the north Atlantic routes, one day I was on a flight from London to New York. The date escapes my memory, but I believe it was in 1989, a few years before my retirement. Shortly after we leveled off at cruise altitude and I made the announcement giving our flight route, weather en route, etc., a flight attendant came up and said, "There is a gentleman in the cabin whose name is Bob Ashley. He wants to know if you are the Bill Travis who was in the 4th Armored Division Band, and if you remember him."

I said, "Of course I remember him, he was one of my best friends in the army," and said to tell him I would come back to talk to him on my break.

It may have been about 30 years later, but I remembered Bob well; a very intelligent guy and a superb classically-trained pianist. When we formed a small band on the side, he quickly learned to play jazz, and we were in various bands together for a couple of years.

We formed a 5-piece band to play for dances, but none of the band members wanted to do job bookings, so I volunteered to be the band leader and do the bookings. I had to go to the various clubs and sell the owner on hiring our band, and make sure we were all there on time to perform. It was my first experience at being a band leader, and that served me well in later years when I had my own 17-piece dance band and a smaller 7-piece party band.

When I took my break, I went back to see Bob and we were able to spend about fifteen minutes chatting and catching up. Bob said that he was coming back from London where he had been working on his production, *Perfect Lives*, an American opera in seven episodes, which has since been seen at film and video festivals around the world. *Fanfare Magazine* called it, "...nothing less than the first American opera...."

After our army days, when we played jazz and dance music together, Bob went on to become a truly distinguished producer and composer of contemporary music. Writing almost exclusively for opera, Bob's career had given him an international reputation

Rick, Clarinet; Bob Ashley, Piano; John, Bass; Lyle, Guitar; Bill, Drums

for originality. In fact, *The Village Voice* commented, "…When the 21st Century glances back to see where the future of opera came from, Ashley, like Monteverdi before him, is going to look like a radical new beginning…." With other statements in the media comparing Bob to everyone from Stockhausen to Wagner, he really was lauded as one of the great American composers.

It was a real treat to see Bob again after so many years, and I'm proud to include my long-time friend, Robert Ashley, in my list of celebrities who were on my flights.

Charles Lindbergh

We had been at cruise altitude for about an hour, on our way from Fairbanks, Alaska, to Tokyo, Japan, when a young flight attendant came into the cockpit and said, "There's a gentleman in first class who says he's a member of the Pan Am Board of Directors, and would like to come up to the cockpit. What should I tell him?"

The captain turned and said, "What's his name?"

"He said his name is Lindbergh. Is it okay if he comes up?"

"Is his first name Charles?"

"Yes, I think that's what he said."

We looked at each other with astonishment, and I thought, *Charles Lindbergh? On our flight?*

After a brief silence, the captain said, "Yes, tell him we would be delighted to visit with him."

The attendant was young, no more than 21 years old, and obviously didn't know who Charles Lindbergh was. She was doing her job correctly by getting permission from the captain before allowing a passenger to come into the cockpit, no matter that he said he was a Pan Am board member. Of course, she wasn't the only person who wouldn't know who Lindbergh was; in fact, many people from earlier generations in the flight industry who knew of him thought he was dead. He was able to travel around the world without being recognized because he had purposely remained out of the limelight for so many years. People just didn't recognize him.

Charles Lindbergh was a good friend of Juan Trippe's, was on the Pan Am Board of Directors, and served as technical adviser for Pan Am for 45 years. He played a huge role in determining the transatlantic routes, and later pioneered most of Pan Am's Asian routes.

"Hi, I'm Charles Lindbergh," he said, very casually, as he came into the cockpit and shook our hands.

I'll never forget those words because it isn't every day that I'd get to meet one of the greatest aviation pioneers in history—one who is every pilot's hero.

He was 70 years old at the time. His tall frame was not as slim as it was in the early photographs we had all seen. Now, he had thin gray hair with a receding hairline, yet he had a quick, friendly smile. We could have passed him on the street without recognizing him. That's the way he wanted it.

This was in 1972, only two years before his death. He told us he was going to Jakarta, in Indonesia, to work on some routes throughout that area for Pan Am, and would be on that project for nearly a month. He spent about 20 minutes chatting with us, and before he went back to his seat, he was gracious enough to allow us to take some pictures of him with us.

Meeting Charles Lindbergh on that flight was the highlight of my aviation career.

Chapter 19 – Famous Pan Am Pilots

Charles Blair

Among his many aviation accomplishments, Pan Am Captain Charles Blair earned the Distinguished Flying Cross, was a military test pilot, and flew one of the first jet fighter flights over the North Pole. He was a Brigadier General in the Air Force Reserves as well as an author; he wrote *Red Ball in the Sky* and *Thunder Above*, which was made into a British movie.

On Charlie's last flight before retiring from Pan Am, he flew the Round the World route, and his wife, movie star Maureen O'Hara, accompanied him on that trip. I was on the same Round the World route one day behind Charlie's flight. We would bring the airplane in, and Charlie and his crew would take the airplane on to the next layover city. On international flights, after landing, the inbound crew had to proceed through Customs and Immigration, so the paths of the inbound and outbound crew never crossed. Consequently, I didn't have the opportunity to meet either Charlie Blair or Maureen O'Hara.

After retiring from Pan Am in 1969, he started his own seaplane commuter service in the Virgin Islands with 19 sea planes, and he loved to fly some of the flights himself. In 1979, the Grumman Goose he flew from St. Croix to St. Thomas developed engine trouble and crashed, killing Charles Blair instantly. There is a memorial in London's Heathrow Airport that was unveiled by his widow. The memorial constitutes a permanent record of his many achievements.

Wayne Poulsen

Wayne Poulsen was a Pan Am captain who was admired by his fellow Pan Am pilots, for his aviation skills, and for all that he had accomplished in his life for the skiing world and the Squaw Valley area of California.

He was born in 1915, died in 1995, and in 2005 a mountain was named "Poulsen Peak" to commemorate his accomplishments and his contribution as a ski pioneer and Squaw Valley Ski Corporation founder.

Wayne loved Squaw Valley, and spent his life defending its integrity. In 1980, he was elected to the U.S. National Ski Hall of Fame, and in 2004 his wife Sandy accepted a Lifetime Achievement Award from the Squaw Valley Institute on behalf of herself and Wayne.

In about 1943, Poulsen purchased 640 acres from the Southern Pacific Railroad, and moved into a tent in the remote valley with his wife. Later on, they built a house to live in, and he continued buying land until he had accumulated around 2,000 acres.

His vision was to make Squaw Valley into "a mountain community dedicated to skiing as a way of life," and in 1948, he entered into a partnership agreement with Alex Cushing to form the Squaw Valley Development Corporation. Later, Poulsen and Cushing had a falling out because of their different visions.

Cushing went on to develop Squaw Valley as a ski resort, while Poulsen began subdividing and selling the land that he had purchased. The development of Squaw Valley as a ski resort made both of them very wealthy.

During my second year with Pan Am, in 1967, I had the pleasure of flying as flight engineer for Captain Poulsen, and found him to be a great pilot and a true gentleman. I recall having dinner with him and two other pilots at a restaurant in Manila, where he talked about skiing all evening.

Warren Simmons

Warren Simmons was a Pan Am captain and entrepreneur who developed many businesses, and was a success at everything he decided to do. His most famous accomplishment was the development of Pier 39 in San Francisco. What isn't so well known is that he also started the Blue and Gold Ferry fleet in the San Francisco Bay to compete with the Red and White fleet.

Warren flew for Pan Am from 1950 until 1970 when he retired at age 43 to spend more time with his business. Over the years, he made many of his Pan Am pilot friends, who believed in him, millionaires through investments in some of his many ventures.

When I first heard of Warren, he had several restaurants in the San Francisco Bay Area named Tia Maria. We ate at one in Oakland often because the food was excellent. He later sold them, and moved into the lucrative apartment to condominium conversion business; he made a fortune during that era.

I never flew with Warren, but did meet him briefly at one of the annual Pan Am Clipper Pioneer reunions. At that time, he had built a chain of restaurants called Chevy's, which he later sold to PepsiCo. There was a time when there was a shortage of cranberries for margaritas, so he went to Chile and planted thousands of acres of cranberries, and became the world's largest grower and producer of cranberries.

After he retired from Pan Am, he worked for five years to get plans approved to develop a rundown area in San Francisco Bay into Pier 39, as a huge tourist attraction. It was a tough and bitter battle, but he stuck to his guns and finally got the approvals. I believe the pier opened in 1978, and he sold it in 1981.

Prior to when he sold Pier 39, there was a 5-star restaurant where my wife and I would often go to eat. The maître d' brought around fresh fish on a platter for us to choose from, and the Caesar salad that he prepared at our tableside, with fresh dressing, was the best Caesar salad we ever had.

To top it off, he prepared flaming cherries jubilee at our table. It was a spectacular show, and needless to say, the cherries jubilee was absolutely delicious. The only other place where I have had cherries jubilee as good as that was in the First Class section of Pan Am. However, they couldn't prepare it with flames on the aircraft.

After Pier 39 was sold, the restaurant apparently changed hands because the maître d' was let go, and the service and food became mediocre. We didn't go back after discovering the change.

Of course, one can't mention Pier 39 in San Francisco without mentioning the seals that took up residency on some of the docks in 1989. They remained there until November 2009, when they disappeared, but reappeared in 2010. They are a huge tourist attraction, with bleachers built on the pier so people can get a better look.

Chapter 20 –
A310, First 2-Engine Atlantic Crossings

In late 1985 I was awarded a captain position on the A310, which was great because it would get me back to flying the North Atlantic routes to Europe. While flying as captain on the A300, I was flying mostly to Guatemala, Mexico City, and El Salvador, or the Pan Am Shuttle between LaGuardia and Boston, which was fun because I made many take-offs and landings. But I missed the longer European flights, and the pay was better on the A310. It also had the modern computerized cockpit.

Pan Am was an aviation pioneer. Juan Trippe, the founder, had visions, set goals, and worked extremely hard to realize those goals. He was a close friend of Charles Lindbergh, who, as mentioned in chapter 18, became technical adviser and consultant for Pan Am for 45 years, was on the Pan Am Board of Directors, and pioneered many of Pan Am's routes for Trippe. Consequently, Pan Am had many firsts in aviation.

In November 1935, the China Clipper, a Martin flying boat built to Juan Trippe's specifications, began a six-day flight from San Francisco to Manila; that was the first transpacific flight.

In 1939, the Boeing B314, also specially designed and built for Pan Am, inaugurated the transatlantic flight from New York to Lisbon and Marseille.

In 1942, Pan Am made the first successful Round the World flight.

Pan Am was the first airline to order the Boeing 747; it was Trippe's idea, and built to his specification. It was the jet that flew faster and farther than any of the earlier jets. It's well known that Boeing CEO Bill Allen, although he was a friend of Trippe's, didn't want to take on the 747 project because he knew it was an extremely difficult, almost impossible task. But Trippe persisted, and one day outside Trippe's New York office after a series of meetings, according to Trippe's secretary, Evans said, "Okay, if you will buy it, I will build it."

And Trippe said, "If you build it, I will buy it."

They shook hands and the deal was sealed.

During World War II, Pan Am flew millions of miles for the U.S. Government, carrying both cargo and military personnel, and built fifty airports in fifteen countries. These are just some of Pan Am's firsts.

ETOPS

In 1985, Pan Am was first to fly the Airbus A310 two-engine aircraft in ETOPS (Extended Range Operations with two engine aircraft) across the North Atlantic. I'm proud to say that I was among the first group of pilots that flew the A310 during that time, and helped to get the A310 ETOPS-certified.

According to FAA Part 121 operations, two-engine airplanes had to stay within 60 minutes of a suitable airport whether flying over land or water. As a consequence, the three-engine jets became popular because it allowed more direct routes over areas such as the Rocky Mountains. In the 1980s, the jet engines became much more reliable and airlines sought to have the distance from an alternate airport extended, so it would be more economical to fly across the oceans.

To become ETOPS-certified, the airline operations, crews, and engines had to meet certain criteria. Pan Am and its crews had extensive ocean flying experience, so what they needed was to have the Pratt and Whitney engines certified. This was accomplished by flying a pre-determined number of hours without an engine failure.

In the beginning, on our routes from New York to London, we were limited to 60 minutes from a suitable airport. That meant we had to fly north near Greenland and use Sondrestrom (now Kangerlussuaq airport) as an alternate.

As the A310 engines flew more flight hours without failure, the distance was extended, first to ETOPS 75 minutes, then 90 minutes, then finally to ETOPS 120 minutes plus 15%. At 120 minutes we could go straight across from New York to London. In 1988, the ETOPS range was extended to 180 minutes.

The Scary First Time

For many years, all of my over-water flying had been in a 4-engine 707 or 747 aircraft; we never had to worry about where to land if we had one engine fail. We would either return to the departure airport if we had not reached the point of no return, or proceed to our destination if we had passed that point.

With a 2-engine aircraft and new Pratt and Whitney engines, it was an entirely different story. Now we were flying into uncharted territory and had to be constantly aware of our position, and where we would go if we had an engine failure.

Once we were out over the Atlantic, closer to Sondrestrom than Gander, Newfoundland, or Goose Bay, Labrador, we had to use Sondrestrom as the alternate. Yes, that was scary. Not that we were afraid of handling an engine failure. That was no problem. We had plenty of training to be able to fly and land on one engine. The scary part was having to land in Sondrestrom under those circumstances because of the possibility of having to make a missed approach. A missed approach is when the pilot has to abandon the approach and go around to begin again. The pilot would have to go around if they didn't see the runway at the proper point, or if there was some other issue, such as another airplane still on the runway.

The Sondrestrom approach chart provides the following caution:

"Adhere strictly to the prescribed procedure due to high surrounding terrain. Expect moderate turbulence on final approach with winds in excess of 20 knots (23 mph)."

The approach to Sondrestrom is on an easterly heading up a fjord, which is a long narrow body of water in a valley surrounded by steep cliffs. At the end of the fjord is the airport. Beyond and on both sides of the airport are mountains—high mountains.

While the approach and landing is a challenge, pilots are accustomed to dealing with challenges; it just means they have to work a little harder on the approach. It's the missed approach on one engine at that airport that presents the hazard, especially if it's done in very low visibility conditions and moderate turbulence. The procedure is to use a climb gradient of 5% for 2.5 miles, then immediately turn right to 109 degrees (to avoid high terrain), climbing to 4,000 feet, then reverse course back west to the starting point for the instrument landing procedure.

Remember: In making that missed approach on one engine, if it is not flown with precision, the airplane could end up crashing into a mountain. That's the scary part.

Sometimes there may be safer ways to conduct an emergency than the FAA-mandated procedure. Such is the situation when deciding whether or not to land at Sondrestrom. If the weather at Sondrestrom is good, which is not very often, then the landing there might be the best option. However, after considering everything else, the best option could be to return to Goose Bay or Gander in Canada, or proceed ahead to Keflavik in Iceland. Decisions like that would have to be made on a case by case basis, and the captain would have to justify that decision to the Chief Pilot and to the FAA. Fortunately no one had to make that decision.

Chapter 21 –
The Great Storm of 1987 in London

Arriving in the Scotland Area

"Larry, get Paris weather for us, please." We were headed for London, but Paris was our alternate airport. In a couple of minutes Larry, my first officer, said, "Paris has heavy rain with winds gusting to 75 knots."

"Damn, that wasn't forecast!"

I immediately called the purser and suggested she get her cabin prepared early for landing, then have the flight attendants take their seats because, as we began our descent into London, we were going to have heavy turbulence. And, as of right then, we weren't sure if we would land at London or divert to another airport.

When Pan Am flight 53, an Airbus A310, departed New York on October 15, 1987, our expected arrival time at London's Heathrow Airport was six o'clock the following morning. The weather forecast for London was rainy and windy, expecting winds of only 25-35 knots.

Subsequent weather reports received en route showed winds to be picking up, reaching 40 knots, but the forecast remained simply "rainy and windy." As we passed the oceanic check points and proceeded over land near Scotland, we learned that the winds there had already picked up to 60 knots. This was much greater than forecast.

A cold front had just passed, and usually things would begin to clear up after the front passed, but that was not happening this time.

The next report we received showed London winds at 50 knots gusting to 75. What the hell was going on? The wind was coming from the south, and the long runways at Heathrow were easterly, which meant a 90-degree cross wind of 75 knots. Even with my cross wind landing experience from my C-46 days with Zantop, it was too much to attempt safely.

The problem facing us was the fact that the weather at our alternate airport, Paris, was as bad as Heathrow. Scotland wasn't any better, and Keflavik was too far to go back. It didn't make sense to try for Amsterdam or Brussels because they were in the path of the weather system and could probably be just as bad when we got there.

"Skipper, here's the latest London weather: Heavy rain, visibility five miles, wind southwest 50 knots gusting to 75; landing runway 23."

"Thanks, Larry, that's wonderful news!"

Okay, I know you're thinking: What's wrong with this guy? That weather sucks. Agreed, it was terrible weather, but with the wind straight down runway 23, we could land in those conditions. It wouldn't be comfortable; in fact, it would be damned uncomfortable, but we could land, and land safely. So it really was wonderful news.

As we descended into the London approach area, the air became extremely rough, so I made an announcement for all flight attendants to take their seats for the remainder of the flight, and for passengers to remain seated with their seat belts fastened.

"Ladies and gentlemen, I've asked our flight attendants to take their seats because it will be very bumpy for the rest of the approach, and I don't want any of them to fall and get injured. It will be very windy for the landing, and because of the strong winds, we won't try to make a smooth landing. Instead we'll strive to make a very safe landing, which means that when I get close to the ground, I'm going to plant the airplane firmly on the runway, and make sure it stays there; it's the safest way in these conditions."

"Clipper 53 London, cleared to hold northeast at Lambourne VOR, 1-minute pattern, descend in holding pattern to 9,000 feet."

"Roger, Clipper 53 cleared to hold Lambourne 1-minute pattern, descend in holding to 9,000. Request 3-minute patterns due to turbulence."

"Clipper 53 London, cleared to hold 3-minute patterns."

"Cleared to hold 3-minute patterns, thank you, Clipper 53."

Larry was on top of it. The air was very turbulent; one minute patterns would have us in almost a continuous turn in the rough air, and was worse on the passengers. Through breaks in the clouds we could see six more airplanes in the same holding pattern below us. We weren't the only ones caught up in this terrible weather that morning.

"Holy shit, Skipper, look at that wind. We're showing 150 knots on our computer here at 9,000 feet; no wonder it's so frickin' rough. I feel like I'm getting my teeth jarred out of my head," said Larry.

"Clipper 53 London, expect approach clearance time 06:45."

"Understand Clipper 53, expect approach clearance time 06:45."

"Dammit, another 30 minutes holding in this turbulence, I sure hope we don't get any passengers sick."

"Ladies and gentlemen, we've been informed that our expected approach time is at six forty-five, so we expect to have you on the ground at seven o'clock. I apologize for the delay, but due to the strong winds, Heathrow is only using one runway for landings, and that's causing traffic to get backed up. I know it's uncomfortable for you, and the best way to deal with it is to sit back in your seat and try to relax your body. We'll have you on the ground shortly."

All I could do was hope the passengers would relax, because then the bumpiness would be a lot easier to tolerate.

"Clipper 53 cleared for approach runway 23, change to tower 118.5."

"Cleared for the approach runway 23, Good day, Clipper 53."

"Heathrow tower, Clipper 53 with you."

"Good morning Clipper 53, report field in sight."

"Clipper 53, field is in sight."

"Cleared to land Clipper 53, wind 230 at 65 knots peak gusts 85."

"Clipper 53 cleared to land."

"65 to 85 knots! Damn, if it gets any stronger we'll be going backwards," Larry remarked.

"Larry, complete the landing check by yourself please, and keep an eagle eye on me. If you see anything you don't like, yell 'go around' and I won't hesitate."

That was an unusual request. I was asking Larry to complete the landing check and verify the completion himself, without using the normal challenge and response procedure. The normal method is for the first officer to call out each item on the check list, and for the captain to look to verify that the item has been accomplished, and verbally respond to the challenge.

On this approach, in moderate to heavy turbulence, I was busy keeping my eyes on the airspeed indicator to keep our ever changing airspeed under control, monitoring the vertical descent indicator for the rate of descent because a rapid rate of descent would occur as the wind gusts dropped off, and I would have to correct that immediately. I also had to monitor to make sure we didn't get below the glide slope. In order for me to make sure that I kept the airplane flying safely in those heavy turbulent conditions, I had to trust Larry to get the check list completed on his own. I knew Larry was quite capable.

"We'll add 25 knots gust correction for the approach speed, Larry. With these winds I'm not going to risk a wind shear problem. We have plenty of runway so I'm not concerned about carrying the extra speed."

"200 feet above the ground, speed is good, watch the sink rate," Larry said, as he continued to monitor the approach instruments to back me up.

"Thanks."

"100 feet."

"50 feet, hold it steady, Skipper, you're doing fine."

"20 feet."

"10 feet."

Touchdown.

I planted the wheels firmly on the runway, and the rain on the runway cushioned the force so it felt rather smooth. Landing on a runway with heavy rain can present the risk of hydroplaning, which is when the wheels are riding on top of the water and can't get sufficient traction for the brakes to be effective. Fortunately, the A310 auto brakes are designed to counteract that very tendency, and with the strong head wind, I wasn't concerned with being able to stop.

"Speed brakes," Larry called out, noting that the speed breaks had automatically deployed to help the airplane slow down. Speed brakes are the flap-like panels, just above where the flaps are located, which, by protruding into the air, assist in slowing the airplane.

"Reverse thrust," I called out as I began to pull back on the reverse levers.

"Manual braking," I called out to alert Larry that I had released the auto brakes and was now using manual brakes.

We came to a stop fairly quickly, even before we were halfway down the runway, and I felt like a thousand-pound weight was lifted off my back.

"Better go slow turning off the runway, Skipper, so the wind doesn't raise our left wing up."

"Right, thanks."

We made a right turn off the runway and taxied slowly and carefully to the terminal, with the airplane still constantly being jostled around by the strong winds. We made it to the terminal safely, and all of the passengers said "thank you" to us as they disembarked from the airplane onto the Jetway.

"Skipper, I'll buy you a beer for breakfast—maybe two!"

"Larry, thank you for a superb job. I was able to relax and concentrate on flying the airplane, knowing you would take care of everything else."

Everyone was surprised by the severity of this storm, but I decided to take all of the weather documents that were provided to us in New York to the hotel with me. I needed to review that weather package to see if there was anything I might have missed. Did I misread any of the weather information? Should I have known earlier, and landed in Keflavik? Once we were in the Scotland area, it was too late to turn back to Keflavik, so I needed to make sure I didn't miss something. After reviewing all of our weather information, and hearing that everyone else was blindsided by the weather, I was confident that I had not made an error.

It turned out to be a fault in the weather forecasting computer models and forecasting techniques. There was a warm air system over the Bay of Biscay to the north of Spain, and a cold system moving down from Iceland. The warm air moved north very quickly for a low of that small size, and when it collided with the cold air it created exceptionally strong wind conditions that the weather forecasters weren't able to accurately forecast.

The local weather forecasters repeatedly forecast only heavy rain, so the London population was not prepared for the extremely high winds that created extensive damage on the ground, causing some loss of life. Winds in parts of southern England reached hurricane forces in excess of 100 knots, and part of the stricken south was devastated.

After that storm, there were modifications made to weather forecasting computer models, and additional training requirements were developed for forecasters. There were additional reporting requirements put in place to provide much better reports about severe weather.

Runway 23 was closed in 2002. It was fortunate for us that runway 23 was still in operation for our arrival on October 16, because we were unknowingly caught up in the "Great Storm of 1987." Had runway 23 been closed during that great storm, we may have been in deep trouble.

Chapter 22 – Unscheduled Landing at Islip, NY

Nice, France, to New York

"Ladies and gentlemen, this is Captain Travis and I would like to welcome you aboard Pan Am flight 83 from Nice to New York. Our flying time will be 9 hours and 5 minutes and we expect to arrive in New York at 4:35 p.m. The weather en route is good, and the weather at New York is forecast to be raining. We'll talk to you again after we reach our cruising altitude. In the meantime, sit back, relax, and enjoy the flight."

Raining was an understatement because the forecast was for thunderstorms with gusty winds, although we did not expect anything like the winds of the Great Storm of 1987 in London. But the word thunderstorms can sound frightening to passengers, while thunderstorms to pilots are just another small challenge, and we try to go around them. Strong, gusty winds are another small challenge that we are quite capable of dealing with; however, we want our passengers to be comfortable; we don't want them to worry about the weather, so we soften the language.

We were on an Airbus A310 with a two-pilot crew plus a relief pilot because the scheduled flight time was over eight hours. I flew the first leg, the first officer handled the radio communications with air traffic control, and the relief pilot provided a third pair of eyes and communicated with Pan Am Operations. We had sufficient fuel to go to JFK, make a missed approach, proceed to Islip, our alternate airport, and then fly for 45 minutes, which is the minimum required fuel. In addition, we had added an extra 60 minutes of fuel that would allow for holding, which was to be expected with these weather conditions. Everything was by the book and we were prepared for anything. The flight en route to New York was uneventful. It was when we began our descent into the John F Kennedy airport area that things got exciting.

Arriving in the JFK Approach Area

"Clipper 83, this is Kennedy approach control, cleared to Sandy Point, descend to flight level 150 (15,000 feet)."

"Roger Clipper 83, cleared to Sandy Point, FL 150, we're leaving FL 250."

"Clipper 83, Kennedy approach, hold Sandy Point FL 150."

"Roger Clipper 83, hold Sandy Point FL 150."

I turned to the relief pilot. "Jim, contact Pan Ops and let them know we're holding."

"Will do, Skipper."

Next, it was the first officer's turn. "Bob, we want to make sure to stay out of any of the heavy thunderstorm cells, so just go ahead and ask them to vector us when necessary."

"Okay, Skipper, consider it done."

"Clipper 83, Kennedy approach, descend to FL120, cleared to Hampton and hold."

"Roger Clipper 83, descending to FL120 to Hampton and hold."

During inclement weather conditions, the number of airplanes that can land and take off each hour at a busy airport is reduced. Therefore, during peak traffic hours such as in the late afternoon, with many airplanes arriving at the same time, the traffic gets backed up. It's sort of like merging onto an extremely crowded freeway during traffic rush hour; the traffic is stop and go.

Obviously, airplanes can only slow down so much without falling out of the sky, so instead of stopping, they're placed into a holding pattern where they fly a two-minute elliptical pattern; that is, they arrive over a navigation fix, then make a right 180 degree turn and fly in the opposite direction for two minutes, then make another 180 degree turn and fly back to the navigation fix.

"Clipper 83 approach, descend to 10,000 feet, cleared to Erick intersection and hold southeast."

"Roger Clipper 83, descending to 10,000 feet to Erick intersection; hold southeast."

"Clipper 83, request direct to Calverton VOR to avoid the heavy cell near Erick."

"Okay, Clipper 83, cleared direct Calverton descend to 10,000 feet, hold Calverton northeast."

"Roger Clipper 83 cleared to Calverton, hold northeast, descending to 10,000."

"Ladies and gentlemen, we're descending to 10,000 feet now, and it looks like we may be landing at about 5:10. The approach will be bumpy because of the rain showers, so be certain to keep your seat belt fastened."

"Jim, get Islip weather and advise Pan Ops we're getting low on holding fuel, and to be prepared in case we have to divert to Islip."

"Here's the weather, Skipper, Islip is 500 ft. overcast, visibility 3 miles, wind 100 degrees at 30 knots with gusts to 45."

"Thanks, Jim, we have 25 minutes of the extra reserve fuel left. The approach to JFK will take 15 minutes once we're cleared, so we can hold for only ten more minutes. Advise Pan Ops again. Also advise the purser that we may have to divert to Islip."

In this type of weather I wanted to be absolutely certain that if we diverted to Islip we would have the full 45 minutes reserve in case we had to make a go around there. Bob had already advised JFK approach that we were reaching the point where we could not continue the approach to JFK.

"Clipper 83 cleared to Deer Park, descend to 4,000 feet, hold southeast; expect approach clearance time 5:35."

That was it, we would not be able to go to Deer Park and hold because it would take us below the minimum fuel.

"Clipper 83 unable to accept; request radar vector for approach to Islip."

"Understand Clipper 83, turn left to 180 degrees, descend to 3,000 feet and contact Islip tower frequency 119.3."

"Roger, Clipper 83 turning to 180 descending to 3,000 feet. Good day."

Due to the length of time we were holding, I had been communicating with the passengers and at one point I advised them of the possibility we may have to go to Islip.

"Ladies and gentlemen, the holding delays are continuing, and we now have to divert to Islip so we can maintain our safe fuel reserve. It's raining at Islip with gusty winds so the approach will still be bumpy. Once we're on the ground we expect to refuel and continue on to JFK."

"Clipper 83 Islip tower, cleared for approach, ceiling 500 feet with rain, visibility 3 miles, wind 100 degrees at 30 knots gusting to 45."

"Roger, Clipper 83 cleared for approach."

This was a significant cross wind. The runway heading was 60 degrees and the wind was from 100 degrees, a 40 degree cross wind on a wet runway. With my early Zantop training in the C-46, which is the most difficult airplane to land in a cross wind, the cross wind didn't concern me. What I had to focus on was the wet runway and the gusts.

If the wind was at 45 knots and dropped off to 30 knots, then the airplane would lose about 15 knots of speed immediately, or lose altitude trying to keep the speed. That could have been dangerous. Our procedure was to add one half the gust factor to our airspeed, which in this case was rounded to 8 knots, which meant I would be shooting the approach approximately 8 knots too fast. Under these conditions I usually added the full 15 knots to our airspeed. Therefore, if the gust dropped off and I lost 8 knots airspeed, all I had to do was lift the nose slightly to hold the altitude, and my airspeed would not drop below my approach speed. Then as the gust came back, the airspeed would increase again. It prevented having to jockey the throttles so much to maintain the minimum airspeed, and made flying the approach much easier and safer.

The potential problem with that procedure was that we could have landed 15 knots too fast. However, with a 7,000-foot runway, there was ample stopping distance even on a wet runway. The key was to be sure to land within the touchdown zone as close to the 1,500 foot marker as possible. It was much safer than the risk of losing airspeed to below the minimum, with a resultant loss in altitude.

"500 feet, Skipper, I see the lead-in lights," said Bob. "Now I have the runway in sight."

"Thanks, Bob, I also have the runway in sight."

"400 feet, speed good, on glide slope," said Bob.

"300 feet, speed low, check the sink rate, Skipper; it's too high!"

"Okay, thanks."

"200 feet speed and sink okay."

"100 feet, doing good."

"50 feet."

"10 feet."

Touchdown.

The approach was very bumpy. I knew the passengers were uncomfortable, but we worked hard to keep the plane on speed and glide path so we could make the approach and landing as smooth as possible. Under these conditions a pilot should not try for the highly desired "grease job" landing. They'd want to plant the airplane safely on the ground at the designated touch down spot so they could stop before the end of the runway. A wet runway will normally cushion a landing, so our landing, while not a grease job, was relatively smooth, and very safe—that was the goal.

Number One Engine

We had to wait about an hour until the thunderstorms were far enough away from the airport that the airport officials would allow airplanes to be fueled. During that time, I walked through the cabin and talked to the passengers to reassure them. We thought things would be routine after refueling and getting ready to go, but man, were we in for a surprise. It was going to be a long, long, long day.

Finally, we were refueled and ready to head for JFK. "Turn number one," was the command to start number one engine.

"We have ignition," said Bob, and within a couple seconds we should have had light up, meaning the engine was starting.

"No light up; aborting start."

We let the engine spool down and tried again—no light up again. Apparently the engine was not getting fuel. After five minutes we gave it another try—still no light up. *Oh shit, now we're in trouble.*

Here we were in Islip. We had been on the airplane for 12 hours, the number one engine wouldn't start, Pan Am did not have mechanics at Islip, and there was no Customs office there. I called Pan Ops, who said the only thing they could do was send mechanics over from JFK, and it would take 1.5 hours to get them there. I asked if we could get the passengers into the terminal and off the airplane for a while. Pan Ops called Customs, who said the passengers must stay on the airplane.

"Well, can Customs send an agent to Islip so our passengers can deplane, get Customs clearance, and go home from here?"

Again Customs said NO. Passengers must stay on the airplane and clear Customs at JFK.

This was going to be an even longer night. The passengers were already upset that we had to land at Islip, and while we had been there the flight attendants had worked hard to keep them happy by serving them the rest of the food we had on board. Then I had to tell them the bad news.

I decided that I had to handle this head on, and speak to them so they could see me, where I could look them in the eye as I spoke. So I went into the cabin, got the purser's microphone, and stood in front of them to give the bad news. Before I went to talk to them, I instructed the relief pilot to go into the terminal to coordinate with Pan Ops on the telephone. The first officer was to stay in the cockpit to monitor the radios, and to leave the cockpit door open to allow passengers to come into the cockpit to visit.

I informed the passengers that because our engine wouldn't start, and we had no mechanics at Islip, Pan Am was sending mechanics, and that, unfortunately, Customs would not allow anyone to get off the airplane. Then I invited anyone to visit the cockpit for a tour if they wish, and said that I would be in the cabin to personally answer any questions.

This was one of those times when the flight attendants needed all the support they could get from the cockpit crew, otherwise some of the passengers would get irate with them. By assigning the first officer and relief pilot specific duties, it left me free to coordinate all the activities and remain in the cabin as much as possible to keep tensions down. Some inconsiderate passengers can become very rude and obnoxious with the flight attendants, but they have to think twice when they're dealing with the captain. I worked my ass off for my passengers, but I wouldn't take any crap.

As I spoke with the passengers, one complained that we didn't have mechanics on standby in Islip. I had to explain that we almost never landed here, so it was not practical to have mechanics there doing nothing. And besides, not only was a landing at Islip very unusual, but to land for fuel and then have a maintenance problem was virtually unheard-of.

One gentleman was traveling with his wife and elderly father; he told me that his father was very ill and needed to go into the terminal. I had the first officer call to see if Customs would give permission. Customs said yes, the man could get off, but had to go by himself; his fellow travelers could not get off with him. When I informed the man of Customs' decision, he said their father was okay to remain on the airplane! I spoke with the father to confirm that he was okay, and he said he was. It was just an attempt on this man's part to play the system. It didn't work.

Finally, the mechanics arrived and found that there was a defective part for which they did not have a replacement. It would have to come from JFK the next day. At that point, things were really getting serious. There was no way we could keep these people on the airplane all night. I had the relief pilot come back and stay in the cockpit, and had the first officer replace me in the cabin, talking with the passengers, while I went into the terminal so I could talk on the phone with Pan Ops in private.

I told them that we were out of food, the passengers were hungry, tired, and angry, and the smokers were having nicotine fits; we had to get them off the airplane. Pan Ops called the Vice President of Operations, who contacted Customs and informed them that we were going to take the passengers off the airplane and bus them to JFK to be cleared. Customs balked, but they had no choice. They were told what was going to happen. Pan Am was not going to keep these passengers on the airplane all night. The VP authorized me to order enough pizzas—the closest food to the airport—for all the passengers, and it looked like we could get them delivered before the buses arrived.

A short time later, the bus company dispatcher contacted me to coordinate, and said he would have one bus there in 30 minutes and the other two in an hour and a half, maybe sooner.

He said, "The one bus will drive up to the airplane and take as many passengers as will fit."

I said, "No, sir, that won't work. The passengers will kill each other trying to get on the bus first. The only way it can be done is to drive up with three buses at one time and take all the passengers."

He said, "I'm not gonna just let one bus driver sit there for another hour doing nothing."

"Listen to what I'm telling you, sir. These passengers are exhausted, and extremely irritable. If you only bring one bus to the airplane we will have passengers fighting to get off first. I cannot allow that to happen."

So in his loudest, gruff, New York dispatcher voice, attempting to intimidate me, he yelled,

"That's your problem cap'n; I ain't gonna let my bus driver sit doin' nuthin'."

So I just lowered my voice and said, very slowly,

"Sir, you're not hearing what I'm telling you. Listen carefully this time. Do not bring only one bus to my airplane. I don't care how you arrange it, but you can only approach my airplane when you have three buses ready. If you bring only one bus anywhere near that airplane I will personally kill the driver. Do you understand what I'm telling you? If you don't understand, then I'll have the Vice President of Operations call and explain it to you in plainer English. Now, before I hang up, do you understand my instructions, or should I have the Vice President call you?"

"Okay, I got it."

"Great, thank you for your cooperation, goodbye."

There was a person in the terminal working for the fixed base operator who was servicing the airplane. He was our ground contact, so I told him, "Make sure when the first bus gets here to keep it out of sight, and don't let it near the airplane until all three buses are here."

"Yes, sir, I'll take care of it."

It was 11:00 p.m. by this time and we had been on the airplane for about 19 (yes, nineteen) hours. I went back to the airplane and informed the passengers that we finally had good news. Pizza and buses were on the way! With that news, the cabin broke into applause. Not applauding me, but applauding the news that they would soon be off the damn airplane. There was a separate crew bus coming for the crew.

The three buses and pizza arrived at about the same time, so we put the pizzas on the buses for the passengers and some on the crew bus for the crew. The entire crew lined up on the stairwell to assist the passengers down safely because the stairway was wet, and also because we wanted to thank them for their understanding and patience during the ordeal. All but a couple of the passengers were understanding and thanked us for keeping them informed, and trying to keep them comfortable. One couple got off uttering,

"We'll never fly Pan Am again!"

Well, you can't please them all.

On the crew bus, on the way to JFK, we started eating our pizzas, and one of the flight attendants said,

"A beer would sure go good with this."

I said, "Why not? I think we deserve it, and you guys were so fantastic, it's my treat."

We had the crew bus driver stop at the nearest place where we could get a beer. A bar! I took off my jacket and shirt epaulets, two flight attendants took off their jackets, and we went into the bar—not exactly incognito—to order take-out. We explained our situation to the bartender, who broke his rules by selling us beer to take off the premises. I guess he could see how tired and thirsty we were—or maybe it was because the two flight attendants had purposely unbuttoned the top of their blouses to show some cleavage.

We were supposed to go directly from the airplane to Customs, and Customs would have been upset if we didn't—but the beer tasted good and since we were exhausted, we really didn't care. However, before we got to Customs, I asked everyone to fill out their Customs forms so I could take them all inside by myself. I figured the beer smell from one person wouldn't be too bad, but ten people would smell like a brewery. When we arrived at JFK, I went to the Customs desk and approached the Customs agent, who appeared tired from waiting for us because his shift had been over several hours ago.

I said, "Sir, if you don't mind, my crew is exhausted from having been on that damn airplane for over 19 hours, and since no one has anything to declare, I thought it would save you some time if I brought these forms in for everyone."

To my surprise, he just took the forms and said, "Have a good evening." He was as anxious to get out of there as we were.

Chapter 23 – Hong Kong Kai Tak Airport

Kai Tak was Hong Kong's international airport until 1998. Built on reclaimed land at the tip of the Kowloon Peninsula, the single runway jutted out into Victoria Harbor and ran roughly from east to west. On the eastern side of the runway, and all along the south and immediate north side of the runway is Victoria Harbor. The north and the west sides are surrounded by hills and mountains, which leaves very little margin for error. The final approach, from west to east for runway 13, was over a large number of low rise buildings surrounded by higher buildings. To get to the runway was like threading a needle at 200 miles per hour. In fact, a program on the History Channel a few years back ranked Kai Tak at number six in a top ten list of extreme airports.

The approach to runway 13 at Kai Tak was spectacular, world-famous, and potentially dangerous if a pilot screwed up. To me, it was the most challenging and exciting approach in the world, and every pilot who flew the Pacific loved that challenge and excitement. The people on the ground under the final approach apparently loved the excitement too, because they expressed sadness when Kai Tak closed.

The turn onto the final heading for the approach had to be done with precision, while also controlling airspeed and altitude. There was little room for error. The video in the link below shows a number of rough landings at Kai Tak. It's well worth watching. http://www.youtube.com/watch?v=3PCOcyt7BPI&feature=related

Photo by Bill Travis

There were several accidents with fatalities over the 70+ years before Hong Kong's international flights switched to the new Chek Lap Kok airport in 1998. Now, the terminal and other buildings have been razed, and all the low buildings in the final approach path were demolished to make room for high rises.

Long Duty Days

When I flew into Hong Kong, it was on the Pan Am Boeing 747 that flew non-stop from San Francisco, although sometimes due to strong winds we had to stop at Taiwan for extra fuel. We had a double crew because the duty time would be up to 14 hours. The flights would leave San Francisco late in the afternoon, so the time we were actually awake would be much more than 14 hours, actually closer to 24.

Obviously, when we arrived at Hong Kong, we were not at our peak physical or mental state, but we had to perform at our highest level. With the double crew, we were able to get a rest break on the airplane in the bunks just behind the cockpit, and that helped. The runway 13 approach required advance planning, alertness, crew coordination, and team work—it helped to be rested.

Precision is the Key to Success

To make a successful approach and landing on runway 13 in low visibility and/or strong cross wind conditions, the Pan Am pilots had to know exactly what actions to take at each step during the approach, and make sure their thought process was several miles ahead of the airplane, anticipating each upcoming action. Getting behind the airplane in the thought process would almost surely guarantee a rough landing.

Visualization

This is where reviewing the approach while at cruise altitude, and taking the time to visualize the entire approach, seeing myself maneuvering the airplane to a good, smooth, safe landing was so valuable. It would assure me that I would be ahead of the airplane because I had just flown the approach in my mind.

The Runway 13 Approach

The approach procedure began over Cheung Chau Island heading west. After crossing the island, I would make a right turn back to the east to intercept the localizer to guide me to the point where I would see the runway. However, the runway would be on my right, instead of straight ahead like all other airport approaches.

After intercepting the localizer, I would descend to cross the outer marker, which was five miles out, at 1,800 feet.

At the outer marker, I would descend to the minimum altitude of 675 feet, and continue on the localizer to a point just 2.2 miles from the runway.

All this time, I would be looking straight ahead for a large red and white checker board painted on the side of a small mountain—an unsubtle but useful aid to navigation. I would also be looking for white flashing strobe lights and lead-in lights ahead and to my right, but these were before the checker board; I never went as far as the checker board, or I would be in big trouble. That mountainside checker board was just a point to aim for until I saw the lead-in lights. The whole approach depended on these visual cues. The situation of runway 13 meant that an instrument landing was out of the question; it was all down to visibility and pilot judgment.

When I saw the white strobes, I would begin the descent, and a turn, so as to stay just inside the lead-in lights. After beginning the turn, the runway would come into view. By staying slightly inside the curving lead-in lights, the course corrections were easier. The descent rate, airspeed, and the turn rate had to be coordinated so that I was lined up with the runway by 200 feet above the ground. Once I had accomplished that, the rest of the approach and landing was routine, except that I was going over the tops of buildings all the way to the end of the runway, and when I banked the wing to the right to turn, it looked to the passengers like the wing tip would touch the rooftops.

Visual Glide Slope Lights

Finally, since this was one of the most complicated approaches in the world, the airport authorities added some visual glide slope indicators on each side of the runway to provide more assistance to the pilots. They consisted of a set of four lights at the target touch-down point, 1,500 ft. from the runway threshold. I would be watching these lights and using them as a visual glide slope indicator while I made the turn onto the final approach heading. If all four lights on both sides were white, I was too high. If the inner two lights were red and the outer two lights were white, I was on the visual glide path. If all the lights were red, I was too low, and had to make a correction to prevent landing short. Landing short could be extremely embarrassing, and at best, could result in early retirement.

Missed Approach Procedure

As the whole approach depended on visibility, if I didn't see the runway by the 2.2 mile point, I would have to immediately climb to 4,500 feet, and at the middle marker—1.6 miles from the runway—make a right turn to intercept a navigation radio bearing, and continue the missed approach procedure. The missed approach procedure had to be executed right at the 2.2 mile point because there were mountains dead ahead of us—mountains and a Boeing 747 do not make a good combination.

The Consequences of Overshooting the Turn

Overshooting the turn for the final approach could set me up for a lot of extra work, and probably a hard landing with potential damage to the landing gear, engine pods and wing tips—or worse, leave me in the harbor at the end of the runway. If I was late turning, then naturally I would overshoot the final heading. That would leave me with a corrective turn back to the desired flight path. Then, as I got back to that desired path, I'd have to make another corrective turn to capture the path. By that time I would almost be at touch down point, where any error could be magnified tenfold.

If there was a cross wind, the problem was greatly exacerbated because I would not only be having to make that turn to correct and line up with the runway, but also had to make the cross wind correction to make sure the airplane lands heading straight down the runway. The aircraft could tolerate a lot of stress, but after a hard landing the mechanics had to perform an inspection to check for damage. I never had to do it, but it must have been embarrassing to have to write up "hard landing" in the maintenance log.

My philosophy was always that it was better to explain to my Pan Am Chief Pilot why I made a missed approach and went around, rather than try to explain why I ran off the end of the runway, and put the airplane and passengers into the waters of Victoria Harbor. However, the strongest motivation for the Pan Am pilots to do it right was that we had the responsibility for the safety and comfort of our passengers.

Overshooting the Touchdown Zone

The majority of the landings at Kai Tak were exciting, but uneventful. Unfortunately, some were not so good. In 1993, a China Air flight was landing with 70 degree crosswinds at 20 knots gusting to 40, and there was wind shear reported, which is a sudden change in wind speed and direction over a short distance that can cause abrupt changes in airspeed and a resultant loss of altitude. According to the reports, the airplane did not touch down within the 3,000 foot touch down zone. If an airplane does not touch down within the touch down zone, it should immediately go around. However, instead of executing a missed approach at that time, the pilot continued to land about 2,100 feet past the touch down zone.

That left less room to stop, and apparently there were a couple of other mistakes made that caused hydroplaning, where the wheels are on top of the standing water on the runway and not getting sufficient traction for the brakes.

He was then on a collision course with the Approach and Landing

System at the far end of the runway, so he elected to ground loop the airplane so it would turn and go off the runway sideways to miss the ALS. There were 22 minor injuries in this accident. About 13 minutes prior to this approach, a British Airways flight had refused to make the same approach because of the current conditions with the reported wind shear.

Sometimes a pilot will take the risk, thinking he may be criticized for going around, or that he may inconvenience the passengers by going to an alternate airport. The intentions are honorable, but the judgment is faulty—and in cases like this, the result can turn out to be disastrous. By refusing the approach under those conditions, and going to an alternate, the passengers would have been inconvenienced, but they would have been safe.

After a successful approach and landing at Kai Tak airport, it was always time to go have a cold one—or two—to relieve the stress, while the pilot who made the landing could brag about how good a grease job it was, and the other pilots could say, "I could have done it better!"

Chapter 24 – My Airline Heroes

Chelsey Sullenberger

In 2009, aviation had a new hero in Captain Chelsey 'Sully' Sullenberger, for landing US Airways Flight 1549 safely in the Hudson River after encountering a bird strike that took out both of the A320 engines. His skill, along with the skill of his crew, saved the lives of many people: those on the airplane, and those on the ground who may have been killed had he attempted another option.

His remarkable feat was accomplished because of the skills he had acquired through his many years of aviation training and experiences. The knowledge of what to do—and how to do it—was ingrained deep in his subconscious mind. It was a matter of calling on those experiences to help him make a rapid decision as to what would be the best course of action. As he weighed the options, he kept heading in the direction that, at the moment, would be the safest—over the Hudson River.

While he was over the Hudson, he could determine if he could make it to LaGuardia or another nearby airport such as the Teterboro airport in New Jersey. Once he decided that the other options were not viable, he was in a position to continue straight ahead where he was able to make the safest landing possible under the circumstances—in the Hudson River. He and his crew received well-deserved national recognition for the outstanding job they did that day.

Dick Ogg

On October 14, 1956, 53 years before the Miracle on the Hudson, Pan Am Captain Dick Ogg successfully ditched a Pan Am Boeing 377 Stratocruiser in the Pacific Ocean, with no loss of lives. Ditching was constantly on the minds of Pan Am pilots because of our extensive overwater operations, and we had trained for ocean ditching. However, the risk of having to ditch was minimized because we had four engines; that is, until the A310 came along.

I recall being on a flight with Captain Ogg the year before he retired, and we had an after flight crew party in Honolulu. After a while, one of the ladies, a young stewardess probably 22-23 years old, said good night—she was going to turn in. Captain Ogg, who was about one year away from retirement, got up and jokingly said,

"I think I'll escort this young lady safely to her room, make my complementary pass, and then go to my room and crash."

Chuck Kimes

On June 28, 1965, 44 years before the Hudson incident, Pan Am had another hero when Captain Chuck Kimes landed an airplane with half of one wing missing, and the number four engine torn off—once again, with no casualties.

Only seconds after take-off, the fire alarm sounded for the number four engine; First Officer Miller looked out his right window to see clouds of thick black smoke coming from the right wing, smoke that prevented him from seeing that the number four engine and part of the right wing were actually missing—not just burning. Either way, he was seeing smoke billowing from the fire in the wing and knew they had a serious problem. Captain Kimes immediately took control of the aircraft, and instructed Miller and Flight Engineer Fitch

Robertson to perform the emergency fire procedure. They did as instructed, but the fire alarm kept sounding.

Pan Am Flight 843 had taken off from the San Francisco airport at 2:09 p.m., and was heading through the "gap" between two mountains just to the south of the city of San Francisco. Captain Kimes found that he was having difficulty keeping the wings level.

Kimes quickly called the tower and announced, "Mayday—Mayday—Mayday," in rapid succession to inform the tower that the aircraft was in a life-threatening situation. The tower immediately placed all other aircraft on hold and informed Captain Kimes that all runways and air space were open to him.

He was only able to reach an altitude of 1,200 feet, and because the wing was slowly disintegrating, with more and more pieces falling off, it was extremely difficult to keep the wings level. He had to make a quick decision:

- Should he go out over the ocean and ditch, which may risk many lives?
- Should he try to go back and land at San Francisco?
- Should he go to Travis Air Force Base in the valley, 40 miles away?

To get back to the San Francisco Airport, he would have to either go west and south, where there was a range of mountains. Or he could go right and try to turn tight enough to stay over the bay; however, the Golden Gate and Bay Bridges were obstacles. A decision had to be made.

Captain Kimes had a deep voice, and was an orator of sorts—a great story teller. After he made his decision, he got on the PA and said to the passengers in a very calm and reassuring manner, as calm as if he were a radio announcer beginning to report the evening news:

"Ladies and gentlemen, this is Captain Kimes. We have a minor problem here…. Well, maybe it's not so minor…. We're going to head for Travis Air Force Base, which is about 40 miles over in the valley, because they have a nice long runway there, longer than San Francisco's runway. Second Officer Max Webb is going to talk with you from here on in, and give you any instructions, because I'm going to be quite busy with the landing."

Our brain operates extremely fast. It's faster than any computer that has ever been built, and probably ever will be built. Our eyes and other sensory organs recognize the problem, transmit the information to our "conscious" mind, which digs into the "subconscious" mind to sort and evaluate the options, and within nanoseconds a decision is made. In the case of Captain Kimes, his subconscious mind, which had stored data from years of experience, training, and visualization of many types of emergencies, quickly provided the correct course of action.

Kimes recognized that ditching in the Pacific Ocean could be a tragic mistake because he was having difficulty keeping the left wing up. He knew from experience and training that as soon as the airplane touched the water, the left wing would probably drop and dig into the water, which would cause the airplane to cartwheel and break up. That would have been catastrophic. I don't know the condition of the seas at the time, but the swells could have been between three and six feet high, and if the airplane hit the swells going the wrong direction, that is, into the major swell instead of parallel to it, that would have exacerbated the problem.

Kimes elected not to ditch, since he was able to control the airplane—although with great difficulty—and decided it was safer to land at Travis AFB. On their way to Travis AFB, Max Webb assisted by pointing out high obstacles in their flight path, such as an 800-foot smoke stack and 800-foot high-tension wires, and did much of the radio communications.

Webb also went into the cabin to help the flight attendants and reassure the passengers. According to an article that Webb later wrote, one man stopped him and asked, "Are we going to make it?"

Webb assured him that they will be all right, but the man wasn't convinced. So Webb said, "You should be taking notes."

"Why?" the man asked.

"So you can remember this all your life."

The man said, "I can do that without notes!"

The aircraft had lost hydraulic fluid from the engine falling off, and since the crew suspected they might have trouble getting the gear down, Webb helped Robertson, the engineer, to crank the gear down manually. They got the gear down in time to avoid a belly landing.

Due to the condition of the aircraft, and the difficulty of keeping it level, the crew didn't know how rough the landing would be; therefore, they elected to instruct the passengers to brace for a crash landing. Captain Kimes was able to line up with the runway, proceed with the approach, and the landing was relatively smooth. When the airplane came to a full stop, the passengers were evacuated immediately and safely.

Captain Kimes was the last one to leave the aircraft and proceed down the chute, where he arrived on the ground to a well-deserved round of applause from all the passengers. The crew noted that the passengers deserved a round of applause too because they had handled themselves extremely well during the harrowing 25 minute ordeal.

Captain Kimes and crew were awarded the Daedalian trophy, an award that is presented annually to the captain and crew of a U.S. commercial airline that has, in the opinion of the Daedalian Awards Committee, demonstrated the most outstanding ability, judgment, and/or heroism above and beyond normal operational requirements during the preceding calendar year.

The FAA also presented them with a service medal for a "masterful feat of airmanship."

When I was a co-pilot on the 707, I had several trips with Captain Kimes and can confirm that he was a superb airman, and an interesting story teller.

Chapter 25 – Problem Passengers

During the earlier years, when flying was luxurious and glamorous, there were fewer problems with passengers than after the mass public began flying with the introduction of the Boeing 747. Today, our society seems to have become disrespectful of authority, and has more of a feeling of entitlement. I never had many problem passengers during my career, but there are a couple of incidents worth sharing.

Just Give Me Another Minute

After dinner, on a flight from Paris to New York, a passenger in Clipper (Business) Class went into the First Class section to sit beside a friend. The purser informed the gentleman that he needed to go back to Clipper Class, that he could not stay there.

He said, "I'll go back in just a minute. Bring me a scotch and soda."

"I'm sorry, sir, but I cannot serve you anything in First Class."

"Bullshit, I'm a Clipper Class passenger, and drinks are included in the fare."

"That's correct; however, you can only be served in Clipper Class. Now please return to your seat."

"Get the hell away from me. I told you I would go back in a minute."

If a First Class passenger wishes to go to Clipper or Economy Class to sit with a friend, that's permissible because the First Class passenger has paid the maximum fare. Economy or Clipper Class passengers cannot move up to other sections because they haven't paid the additional fare.

The purser walked back to the galley to give the man a couple of minutes, then walked back and said, "Sir, you must return to your seat now."

"Dammit, don't you have anything better to do than hassle me?"

"Yes, sir, and you are interfering with my work by refusing to return to your seat."

It became obvious that this passenger wasn't returning to his seat until he was ready, so she came to talk with me. "Captain, a Clipper Class passenger has moved up to First Class to talk to a friend and refuses to move back. He's been there for 15 minutes and has become very rude."

"Okay, I'll have a chat with him."

During those days, the captain could go back into the cabin if a problem was getting out of hand. We would put on our uniform coat, which denotes more authority, and put on our hat, which adds even more authority and also has the effect of making us look taller than we are. It's a psychological thing.

"Hello, Mr. Jones, I'm Captain Travis. I understand that you purchased a seat in Clipper Class, is that correct?"

"Right."

"And I also understand that you've been in First Class for 20 minutes, and refuse to return to Clipper Class."

"I told that woman I would go back in a minute, and she keeps bothering me."

"Yes, sir, I understand, and she's doing her job properly. You paid for a Clipper seat, and you cannot sit in First Class. So I need you to go back to your Clipper seat now."

"I'll go back in just a few minutes!"

"No, sir! You don't understand. I'm saying you must return to your seat now, and if you and your friend wish to continue your conversation, he can go to Clipper Class with you."

"Dammit, Captain, don't you have anything better to do? I keep telling you people I'll go back in just a minute."

"Yes, sir, I have much more important things to do, and I need to get back to the cockpit to do them. Now listen carefully: when you see me open the cockpit door, if you're not standing up and on your way back to your Clipper seat, then you may as well stay in First Class because I will send a message to Pan Am to meet you in New York and charge you for the full First Class fare. Do you understand?"

He looked at me and mumbled something under his breath as I turned around and headed toward the cockpit. As I opened the door and turned around to check, Mr. Jones was headed back to his Clipper seat. We didn't have any more problems with him.

21st Birthday Celebration

Two guys were getting drunk and disruptive in the rear cabin, and the purser cut their drinks off. The birthday kid, who was tall, probably weighed 225 pounds, and was obviously a body builder, was not going to be easy to deal with. He started swearing at the purser and called him a black ass N....., and kept demanding they bring him another drink.

We were midway between London and New York when the purser came to say he was having a difficult time with a young male passenger who was traveling with his mother. The purser told me that the mother had moved to another seat to get away from her disruptive son. The kid had started talking to another young guy across the aisle from him, and they had been ordering drinks from different flight attendants. That way the flight attendants wouldn't know how much they were drinking. But after they began showing signs of intoxication, the flight attendants discovered what they were doing. It seemed it was his 21st birthday and he was going to live it up because he could now legally drink.

At that point, the purser only wanted to advise me of the situation. He wasn't requesting assistance. However, about 20 minutes later, he told me it was getting out of control. The birthday kid was belligerent, yelling at the flight attendants and again called him names, and this time threatening to "beat his ass when the plane landed." I thought this might be a tough situation to handle, and we could end up having to restrain him, so we devised a plan.

I gave the purser a pair of restraining flex-cuffs for himself, and one to give to a deadheading pilot, who was seated in the Economy section. The kid was sitting in the last seat in Economy, which played in our favor because the purser and another male flight attendant could stand directly behind him. The purser was to enlist the deadheading pilot to get behind me when I came back. That way, we would have two male flight attendants standing behind him, then me confronting him, with the deadheading pilot backing me up. A female flight attendant would stand beside the males with a fire extinguisher.

When the large nozzle of a fire extinguisher is pointed at ones face, it's a menacing sight. When one hears a flight attendant yell, "Sit down asshole or I'll freeze your frickin' face," and lets off a blast of the chemical, which emits an ominous, loud sound and very cold, cloudy, dense air, the target of that extinguisher will usually comply. It's crude language, I know, but the misbehaving passenger understands better when you're talking their language. They know you're not pussyfooting around, and they're more likely to comply with your commands.

If they don't comply, then they'll get a blast of ice cold chemical in their face. If that doesn't stop them, then the next thing they might feel is the metal fire extinguisher itself landing upside their head. That was a last resort, and to my knowledge, was never used. There were, however, plenty of unruly passengers restrained by the flex cuffs over the years.

Our goal was to get this kid under control without any physical confrontation, but if he attacked us, we were prepared to end the situation swiftly. We felt that the four males could contain him, while the female with the intimidating fire extinguisher, as a scare tactic, was a good backup.

I put the seat belt sign on and made an announcement, "Ladies and gentlemen we're expecting some clear air turbulence, so please return to your seats and fasten your seat belts."

Then I put flex cuffs in my rear pocket, donned my coat and hat, to look as tall as I could, and started down the cabin aisle. As I walked back, I saw the two male flight attendants moving into place behind the kid, and the female attendant getting the fire extinguisher. The deadheading pilot stood up and followed behind as I passed him.

When I approached the kid's seat, I noticed that neither he nor his friend across the aisle had buckled their seat belt. The kid was slightly slumped back in his seat, which would make it easy for him to kick me in the groin, so when I approached his seat I took a slightly bladed position so he could only hit my leg if he kicked.

"Hello, sir, I understand there is some problem. Can you tell me what's bothering you?"

"I'm not your son, and these cheap assholes won't give me any booze."

"I didn't call you "son." I addressed you as "sir," out of respect, and I expect you to be respectful as well."

"Then tell these assholes that I paid a lot of fucking money for this ticket and I expect service."

"Sir, first of all, the seat belt sign is on, and you need to buckle your seat belt."

"You too, sir," I said to the friend across the aisle.

"I also need both of you to lower your voices and stop using the foul language because you're disturbing my other passengers, who also paid a lot of money for their tickets."

The guy across the aisle said, "Yes, sir, I'm buckling my seat belt, and I won't be causing you any trouble."

"Thank you, sir."

Then I turned back to the kid and said, "Now, sir, buckle your seat belt."

The real purpose of getting him to buckle his seat belt was to establish control. He would still be able to unbuckle it quickly if he wanted to, but once I had control, I didn't expect any more problems.

He apparently sensed that someone was behind him because he turned his head and saw the two males directly behind him, and the female flight attendant with the fire extinguisher in one hand, and holding the large funnel in her other hand, pointed directly at him. He must have quickly realized he was outnumbered, and that we meant business, because he turned back around and reluctantly buckled his seat belt.

"Thank you, sir. Now I have to go back to the cockpit. I need both of you to behave back here. Stop the shouting, don't disturb my other passengers, and don't give my flight attendants any more hard time."

"Okay, but I want another drink."

"No, sir, you're both cut off. I instructed the flight attendants to not serve either of you any more alcohol."

"But I paid a lot of money for this fucking ticket and I expect service."

"You'll get food and beverage service, but you have had too much to drink and you're cut off. No more alcohol."

"That's bullshit!"

"Now listen closely. I'm going back to the cockpit. If my flight attendants report that you're still misbehaving, I won't bother coming back to talk to you again. I'll land this airplane at the closest airport, which right now is Goose Bay, Labrador, where the Canadian police will come onboard, handcuff you, remove you from the airplane, and arrest you. You'll spend the night in a Labrador jail. If you don't believe it, try me."

I had him under control. He was not getting any more alcohol. Standing there arguing with him further, and having him continue to swear, would accomplish nothing but continue to upset the other passengers, and there was a risk that the situation could escalate, which we wanted to avoid. There was nothing else I needed to do at this point. He was under control, so I left him to visualize what it may look like on the inside of a Goose Bay, Labrador jail.

Later, I asked the purser if he wanted to press charges for being physically threatened, which would be the only way we could have police in New York arrest him. He said yes, and I agreed. This kid needed to be taught a lesson. No one calls my flight attendant a "black ass N....," threatens him with physical violence, and gets away with it. So, we had the police meet the airplane in New York.

At the gate, two uniformed officers stood just outside in the Jetway, on each side of the door so one could grab each arm. A few feet down the Jetway, there was another uniformed officer who would catch him if he elected to run. Another officer stood beside me at the cockpit doorway. As the kid came closer to the door, a flight attendant pointed him out to the officer. As he passed me I said, "Goodbye, sir," and the officer got behind him. As he stepped out the door, the officers grabbed each arm, handcuffed him, and took him into custody where he spent the night in a New York City jail.

The purser decided not to press charges—he just wanted to

teach the kid a lesson—so he didn't go to the court house the next morning. I hope the kid used the night in jail to think about the consequences of his actions, and didn't get drunk and belligerent on his future flights.

Chapter 26 – Lockerbie

It was pure luck that Pan Am Flight 103 had a delay at the airport waiting its turn to take off because the altitude and time delay set for detonation of the bomb was planned so Pan Am 103 would be over the ocean when the bomb went off. That way, no evidence would be discovered, and no one would learn the cause of the accident. It was a brilliant plan, but fate played its hand, and while the bombing succeeded, the bombers were caught.

The bombing of Pan Am Flight 103 over Lockerbie has been covered in many writings, so I won't go into detail except to express the feelings of one flight crew in the aftermath.

I knew Jim MacQuarrie, the captain of Pan Am 103, and recognized several names of other crew members. It's always sad when fellow crew members lose their lives in an airplane accident, and the sadness turned to anger when I learned that the accident was the result of terrorism. It also caused me much stress and anxiety as I had to fly another flight the following day, with a load of trusting passengers, from the same airport where the bomb was placed on Pan Am 103.

I was in London on the day the bombing of Flight 103 occurred, and was scheduled for a flight to New York on the A310 the following day. It was a strange feeling, one that I'll never forget. The following day, the crew bus picked up our crew of eleven at the hotel. During the long ride to Heathrow, not a word was mentioned of the bombing, although it was uppermost in the mind of everyone there.

It was such an eerie feeling, from the time we boarded the aircraft, taxied out for take-off, and on into the climb-out phase. We all went about our duties, flying the airplane as we normally would, but in the back of our minds I know we were all thinking about Pan Am 103, and wondering if we were about to encounter the same fate.

There was none of the usual banter, no idle conjecturing, no telling of jokes, no complaining about how badly the CEO was running Pan Am; there was just a deafening silence—broken only by the reading of check lists and communications with air traffic control.

The thought of Pan Am 103 exploding at 31,000 feet, people blown out of the airplane into the freezing sub-zero air, void of life sustaining oxygen, was almost unfathomable. We could only hope that the shock of being violently sucked out of the airplane during the rapid decompression would cause immediate death so they didn't suffer while being plunged to the ground on that fateful day.

It was only after we were out over the ocean, one hour beyond Ireland, that we were finally able to relax.

We didn't realize it at the time, but the bombing of Pan Am 103 not only killed all the people on that airplane, but it was also the final knife thrust into the vital organs of Pan Am—a large contributor to the death of Pan Am some three years later. The picture of that 747 cockpit lying on the ground at Lockerbie, amidst the twisted jagged metal of the wreckage, was so horrific that people were now terrified of flying on Pan Am—the easy American target for terrorists—so much so that they stopped buying tickets for Pan Am flights, causing the airline to die a slow and agonizing death.

Chapter 27 –
Near Miss at 32,000 Feet over Ireland

"Clipper 53 London, report reaching flight level 320." (32,000 feet)

"Roger, Clipper 53 is level FL 320."

"Clipper 53 London, turn right heading 285."

"Roger, Clipper 53 turning right 285," said the captain handling the communications.

"Clipper 53 London, turn further right 295."

"Clipper 53 turning 295."

At this point it seemed like he was just adjusting our heading to vector us to the oceanic check point, but so far it had been a total of 25 degrees, which seemed a bit much. However, we still had no cause for concern since he had not indicated any other reason for the turn.

"Clipper 53 London, turn further right 315 degrees."

"Roger Clipper 53 tur.....," but before the captain could get the words out of his mouth, ATC said, "Clipper 53 turn immediately to 360 degrees."

This was a drastic instruction; now I was concerned. I immediately banked to a little over 30 degrees, the maximum for the autopilot, and thought there must have been traffic out there that ATC hadn't mentioned. As I scanned the horizon I spotted a black dot, about the size of a dime, and as it began to get larger, in the same spot, I knew immediately what it was. I switched off the autopilot, racked the airplane over to a 60 degree bank, and within a second, that dime-sized dot mushroomed into a full size military jet coming at us head on—faster than a speeding bullet!

Adding his speed to ours gave a closure rate of around 1,300 miles per hour, or 1,900 feet per second, which is actually twice as fast as a speeding (9mm) bullet. That doesn't give one much time to duck.

A bank of 30 degrees is the maximum for passenger comfort. A bank of 45 degrees is uncomfortable for passengers, so we never bank that much unless necessary. But on this occasion, I banked to 60 degrees because I had to miss that jet. I would have banked farther if necessary. It was just as I hit the 60 degree mark that it passed us.

A dot moving lower on the windshield of an airplane indicates an airplane at a lower altitude. When the dot moves higher on the windshield, it's at a higher altitude. When the dot stays at the same spot and is getting bigger, it's at the same altitude and coming at the airplane head on. If the pilot doesn't turn immediately, that other airplane is going to ruin the day.

We saw the full underbelly of that military fighter jet as it passed about 100 feet from the left side of our airplane, and I was in the 60 degree bank. The fighter jet must have been in a 90 degree bank to avoid us. Immediately as he passed us, we went through his jet wash causing a huge jolt to our airplane, just as it did when we experienced unexpected clear air turbulence.

The captain keyed the microphone and said, "London, why the hell didn't you tell us you had traffic; you almost killed everyone in two airplanes. We came within 100 feet of that airplane."

"I'm sorry, Clipper 53. That was a military jet that was not being controlled by us. He had no transponder on, so we didn't know his altitude."

"But you saw him on radar, knew he was there, yet failed to tell us that we had traffic. If you had told us we had traffic, then we may have spotted him in time to prevent this near miss. We'll have to file a near miss report."

"Clipper 53, we understand, and we apologize. Turn to heading 285, and you're cleared to oceanic control."

"Clipper 53 turn to 285, and good day."

That was a very brief conversation. Just as it ended, the purser came into the cockpit, very excited, and said, "Captain, what was that airplane we saw? It felt like we hit it."

The captain turned around, and in a very slow, calm voice, said, "What airplane?"

In the event of emergencies and other uncomfortable situations, pilots must remain calm on the outside, no matter how stressed they are on the inside. They cannot allow their inner emotions to surface; otherwise they'll unnecessarily upset the passengers.

In this case, the captain was just momentarily joking with the purser, and so as to not piss her off, he quickly explained what happened, and said, "I'll make an announcement in just a moment—after I check my seat cushion."

Within a couple of minutes, the captain explained to the passengers that the military jet that passed us was flying uncontrolled, and air traffic control had spotted him on radar before we could see him. They had us turn to avoid a collision, and since we were at the same altitude, we passed through his jet wash that created the bump that we felt.

That was all he needed to say. We did not want to overly excite the passengers, and it would not have been prudent to express anger towards Air Traffic Control. He told the truth, but not in a way that would create undue stress to our passengers.

When we arrived in New York, we filed the required near miss report, but never heard about the incident again.

Chapter 28 – Delta Airlines, A Turnkey Route Purchase

The Mad Scramble

"Hello, Jack, I haven't seen you for a of couple years, where have you been keeping yourself?" (Jack was a fellow A310 pilot.)

"Hey Bill, I've been on sick leave for fourteen months with a terrible back problem, but on my visit to the doctor last week, he said I was okay to go back to work."

Later, I was talking to a union rep who said there were five A310 pilots who had been on medical leave for over a year with back problems—a malady that's difficult to disprove—and suddenly, every one of them seem to have been miraculously cured. They were returning to work just in time to get back on the A310 so they wouldn't miss the opportunity to go to Delta. It was called the Pan Am "Miracle Cure."

The Boeing 747 pilots were the most senior pilots in Pan Am. The A310 pilots were the next senior, followed by the Boeing 727 pilots. It was announced that Delta would buy the North Atlantic routes and hire only the pilots who were already checked out on the A310. That way, Delta could immediately begin flying the routes once the sale was consummated. Well, the 747 pilots were enraged by this and fought with the Airline Pilots Association to see that seniority was protected. They called for the union to force Delta to hire the more senior 747 pilots and check them out on the A310. They went so far as to hire an attorney and threatened to sue. But a small group of pilots attempting to fight Delta Airlines would be as futile as taking a knife to a gun fight.

Delta was not about to delay the purchase of the routes because there was intense competition to buy this last remaining piece of prime meat on the Pan Am bones, and Delta needed those routes badly. They also were not going to buy the routes then shut down the North Atlantic operation for several months until all the 747 pilots were checked out on the A310. Shutting down a whole North Atlantic Route system for months would be unthinkable. So, unfortunately, the 747 pilots lost their battle.

The Junior A310 Pilots

"Skipper, have you sat down and given serious consideration as to whether or not it's really cost effective for you to go to Delta Airlines with the North Atlantic Route sale, instead of remaining with Pan Am? After all, the way the seniority merging process is shaping up, you'll lose a lot of seniority numbers if you go with Delta. And just think, once Pan Am gets the $400 million dollar cash infusion from Delta, Pan Am will be out of the woods."

"Yes, Mr. Hyde, I've given careful consideration to the matter, and I will be accepting the offer to go to Delta Airlines with the route sale. But thank you for your *sincere* interest in my financial well-being."

And this is the way it went; all of the remaining Pan Am pilots were turning into raging bulls, fighting to push everyone else out of their way so they could get on the life boats, as the ship was sinking, and be the ones to go to Delta with the North Atlantic Route sale.

Mr. Hyde was my co-pilot on this flight. He and the relief pilot were junior to me, and it was thought that it might be touch and go whether they would be able to go to Delta. Delta needed a turnkey system, so they were hiring the Pan Am pilots who were already flying the Airbus A310—the airplanes used on the Atlantic routes that Delta was purchasing. However, it was not known if Delta would hire all of the A310 pilots, so these guys wanted to convince everyone senior to them that it would be more cost effective for them to remain with Pan Am.

As Terry Bradshaw once said, "I may be dumb, but I'm not stupid."

How could it be more cost effective for me to remain with Pan Am when there would be nothing left but the cleanly-picked bones of a once-great airline—a few remaining South American routes that probably would never turn a profit? In my opinion, the selling of the Pan Am North Atlantic routes was the coup de grâce. It would be only a matter of time before Pan Am was certain to go belly up. I didn't believe Pan Am would ever emerge from Chapter 11—and they didn't. Delta took over the North Atlantic routes on November 1, 1991, and on December 4, 1991, Pan Am ceased operation.

Fortunately, I was in the right place at the right time, and was able to go to Delta. However, we did have to go through a hiring process consisting of filling out the application, having an in-person interview, and attending a four-day orientation where they welcomed us into the Delta family, and issued us their Delta company operations manual.

The Interview

So here I am now with another career-challenging situation. I had to study to make sure that I would pass all of the Delta interviews and tests, so I began to study and envision myself flying the line in the Delta pilot uniform. One potential hurdle to overcome was the Zantop Argosy accident that was on my record. I had to answer yes on the application where it asked if I had ever been involved in an aircraft accident. However, I had several things going for me. Zantop had supported me and provided their attorney to fight the FAA on my behalf. Then Pan Am hired me, knowing about the accident. Pan Am had also recruited me into the training department as a training check captain.

So I visualized myself sitting in the room with the interviewer, who would be a Delta check pilot, telling him about the accident and how the FAA tried to hang me with their ridiculous accusations. I was saying to the interviewer that "the FAA finally dropped their charges, stating that they did not have sufficient evidence to prove their case, and I have the complete record of communication between the Zantop attorneys and the FAA here in my brief case if you would like to review them." I visualized the interviewer saying no.

At the actual interview, when I asked if he would like to see them, he said, "Hell, that was 30 years ago, I don't need to see that stuff. I see your record with Pan Am is exemplary; that's all I need. Welcome to the Delta family."

With that, I donned my Delta Airlines pilot uniform and became a Delta family member. All of this was done prior to the date the sale was effective. This way, on the sale date, the pilots would be ready to fly the North Atlantic route flights as Delta Airline pilots.

I was in New York on the day before the sale date, prepared to go on a Delta flight the following day. As I left the Pan Am terminal to go to my commuter apartment, I noticed that all of the Pan Am signs on the building were draped with large cloths. When I returned the next morning for my flight, dressed in my new Delta Airlines pilot uniform, the cloths were removed, and all the signs on the terminal read "Delta Airlines."

It was a sad feeling, like losing a close friend or family member, but I would go on living and hang on to the memories. It was difficult realizing that Pan Am was gone from the John F Kennedy Pan Am terminal, the futuristic icon that Juan Trippe built.

Delta had a different culture to Pan Am, and we had to get accustomed to that. Also, the Pan Am pilots—in their ongoing efforts to help save Pan Am—had given up over 30% in pay over the past few years. What hurt was that the Delta pilots made about 30% more than us, and when we were hired, we were hired at the Pan Am pay scale. About six months after being with Delta, after they had checked some of their own pilots out as A310 co-pilots, I flew with one of the Delta co-pilots and learned that he was making more money flying as my co-pilot than I was, flying as captain. It stung a little, but I couldn't let that bother me. I had known what the pay scale was when I accepted the job, and had agreed to it; therefore, I would continue to give 100% effort, and greater, to my work.

I always look for the positive side of things, and the positive side of this was the fact that I still had a job—a good job—as a Delta Airlines captain. I was thankful for that.

Unfortunately, many of my fellow pilot friends did not have the opportunity to go to Delta; they didn't have a job—they had lost their livelihoods.

Chapter 29 – The Final Flight

As I reached up into the top corner of the room and tilted my head back slightly, I became so dizzy that I had to get off the chair I was standing on and sit down.

It was a hot humid day in July 1992. I was in my New York commuter apartment where I had arrived the night before in order to rest before taking my scheduled flight to London at six o'clock that evening. During mid-morning, I had begun hanging some wallpaper in the kitchen because my roommates and I had decided we needed to dress the apartment up a little. Self-adhesive wallpaper was much easier than painting.

Within a couple of minutes after sitting down, the dizziness stopped, so I got back on the chair and tried to get the paper to adhere in the corner again. But as soon as I reached up and had my head tilted back, I became dizzy again. The wallpaper had a slight odor so I thought maybe the stuff was toxic, and that I had better stop trying to put it up. Instead of leaving a half-finished job, I pulled all the wallpaper down and discarded it. So much for dressing up the kitchen.

On the flight to London that evening, each time I tilted my head back to reach something on the center overhead panel, I got that dizzy feeling again. What the hell was happening? I'd never had dizzy spells, but every time I tilted my head back to the right, I got dizzy. Then about a minute after my head returned to the normal position, the dizziness disappeared. Well, the way to solve that problem was to not tilt my head back. When I needed something on the overhead panel, I asked the first officer to do it for me. However, I let him know that I was having this problem so he wouldn't be surprised if it developed into something more serious.

On the return flight from London to New York, I experienced the same sensation. Each time I leaned my head back to reach something on the overhead panel, I would get dizzy. Then it would stop a few seconds after returning my head to a normal position. Again I elected to have the first officer reach anything I needed done on the overhead panel, and I made damn sure not to lean my head back when we were on final approach. Normally there would be no reason for me to reach up there on final approach anyway.

After arriving back in New York from London, I continued on home to San Francisco as a non-revenue passenger, and all the way home I kept thinking, *is this way it's going to end? Is this a problem that will end my career just one year short of the mandatory pilot retirement age?*

As soon as I got back to San Francisco, I made an appointment with our family doctor who referred me to an ear specialist. During a one-week period, the doctor put me through every ear test imaginable, both passive and active, to confirm what he thought I had.

Benign Paroxysmal Positional Vertigo

The diagnosis was BPPV. At that moment, I knew my flying career was over, and I didn't get to take the celebratory "last flight," where I could have taken my wife with me to celebrate the 35-year career that she helped me achieve. It was all over except for the formality, which meant I had to take an FAA physical. The doctor giving the FAA physical would note that I had BPPV, and would send this information to the FAA Medical Center in Oklahoma. They would make the final decision as to whether I could pass the physical while I had BPPV.

As expected, the FAA Medical Office sent back a letter denying the physical. Without the physical, my pilot license was no longer valid. I could not fly. My flying career was over. I had flown my last flight as an international airline captain.

The fat lady had sung!

The next formality was to deliver the medical records, and the FAA Medical Office letter, which denied the physical, to the company. Upon receiving those documents, they removed me from flight status and placed me on medical leave.

In order to get back on flight status, the BPPV would have to go away. Then I would have to take the same series of tests again to be sure it was cured, and then take another FAA physical to submit to the FAA Medical Office for approval. By that time it would have been past my mandatory retirement age. But it didn't go away anyway.

This was an event in my life where no amount of visualization was going to help me with my flying career. It was a medical condition beyond my control. Now I would have to begin realizing the after-retirement plans I had been working on for a number of years.

I had to set and achieve new goals.

The Cause

The doctor said this condition was probably caused by the case of bronchitis I had recovered from a few weeks earlier, which had almost developed into pneumonia. It apparently attacked my inner ear, causing some of the tiny calcium crystals (otoconia) to be dislodged from within the utricle section of the inner ear. When the head is in a different position, the displaced otoconia causes the vertigo.

A method the doctor taught me to deal with the situation was to have the inner ear habituate. The procedure was to get my head back into that position, and as soon as the dizziness occurs, raise the head back to normal until the dizziness stops. Repeat that several times at each setting and repeat the sequence several times a day. Soon, the inner ear begins to habituate, or at least sort the conflict out much quicker. It may also reposition the displaced otoconia so the vertigo feeling may not be as strong. This is my layperson explanation; the medical explanations may differ.

Tough Adjustments in Routines

Since I enjoyed several avocations, I was able to adjust to retirement without great difficulty. However, I was accustomed to certain daily routines, and my wife had her own daily routines. Now these different routines were in conflict. We both had to make changes. That proved to be the most difficult.

For the past 28 years, I would be at home for a week or more at a time, with the home routine and responsibilities, and then I would go on a flight, where there was a different set of routines and responsibilities. After being home for five or six days, my subconscious mind, which had been programmed with this routine for all those years, was apparently telling my conscious mind that it was time to go on a flight. But I no longer had a flying job.

It was almost like withdrawal from an addiction.

My wife, on the other hand, was used to me going on a flight after a week or so, at which time she would go about her routine without me being in her way. When I was home, her routine was different than when I was away, so her subconscious would be telling her conscious mind that I would be leaving soon so that she could go about her daily routine.

It was our subconscious minds at work, but we didn't understand what was happening. As a consequence, there were conflicts.

I began to feel that I wasn't welcome in my home. Dee felt that I was an intruder in her home. Apparently, I had been trying to impose my way of running the household, and this interfered with the methods that had worked perfectly well for her all those years. After all, she had raised our four children, managed the home, and kept it spotless, while I was out of the country half the time—a part time father and husband.

It took a while for both our subconscious minds to become familiar with our new life with me being retired; we each had compromises to make. It took some time, but with a lot of love and understanding, we got through that trying period. Today, Dee still runs the household—her way! And, as always, she does it well.

Life without Flying

My flying career spanned 35 years, therefore, it was going to be tough to consider a life without flying. I was going to miss the camaraderie of my fellow crew members, and I would miss watching the beautiful sunsets as we flew west in the evenings—there is nothing like the spectacle of a beautiful sunset as seen from the expansive 180 degree view of the cockpit at an altitude of 37,000 feet. Pilots have always said that we have the best seat in the house—and we do.

Then there was the ritual of watching for Venus, the morning star, to appear, followed by sunrise with the sun glaring in our eyes as we approached our destination after flying all night; seeing the Northern Lights over Fairbanks, Alaska; laughing, joking and telling hangar lies with the crew at after-flight crew parties; layovers at exotic locations; and being able to take my wife on some of my flights, where the flight attendants would treat her like a VIP because she is such a nice lady and was able to relate so well to them.

It was an exciting and rewarding career, but I also had a love for my family and my other avocations. That eased the pain. I had my music, photography, reading, sailing, and other activities that I could now spend more time with. Dee and I were able to do more things together; we both studied photography and would go on photo-taking journeys, and we took sailing lessons and sailed in the San Francisco Bay.

But my big love was music, and for about ten years I had been preparing to get back into music full-time after my retirement. After doing some sailing and other activities, and after my subconscious mind was finally programmed for my new life without flying, I decided it was finally time to go into music as my new full-time job.

Perhaps I should begin that music chapter from the beginning….

Chapter 30 – The Music Scene

Getting Back Into Music

Music has always been a huge part of my life. The interest was nurtured by my mother and my Aunt Sally. When Mother was young, she had a love for music and learned to play the harmonica. Consequently, she wanted me to learn to play a musical instrument, and when I was a youngster she signed me up for guitar lessons. This was in Nashville, the home of country music, and I attended a guitar class with about 20 other young wannabe Grand Ole Opry superstar guitar players. What did I learn? Well, I learned that when you join a large music class, not knowing the first thing about a guitar except that it has six strings, and the class has been in progress for six weeks, there is no way that a new kid will ever catch up and learn anything.

While I loved music, I could see this was going nowhere, so I told my parents I was learning nothing, and they agreed to take me out of the class. They couldn't afford private lessons, so I never learned to play the guitar.

In junior high school, I started playing drums, and the band teacher would coach each student individually; that was the real beginning of my music career. I played in the high school bands and in small dance bands all through high school and after I dropped out of school, until I went into the army where, as I discussed in chapter 7, I eventually got into the 4th Armored Division Band.

After I got out of the army, I played in various bands during college and while studying aviation. Throughout much of my flying career, I would play as often as I could. So, it was only natural that, about 10 years before my compulsory retirement from Pan Am, I had decided I wanted to get into music full-time after retirement. Little did I know that an ear problem would end my career one year earlier than the mandatory retirement date.

In preparation for retirement, I had started taking advanced drum lessons and studying very seriously in between flights—I needed to get my chops back up—and I was fortunate enough to study with a series of world-class players and instructors.

John Xepoleas

http://www.johnxdrums.com, http://www.thefundamentals.com

My first serious drum tutor was John Xepoleas, who has his studio in Pleasant Hill, California. Widely known as John X, he's a great drummer, a superb teacher, and the author of several drum study books. John also has a superb band, The Fundamentals, which has been performing for about 20 years, and has a solid reputation of being one of the San Francisco Bay Area's premier wedding and party bands. Although I was only able to take a few lessons with John, we've kept in touch through my grandson, Anthony.

Anthony has been interested in drums since he was big enough to pick up a drum stick, so a few years ago I introduced him to John X. They had an instant connection, and now John is his instructor and also a good friend. In 2012, when Anthony earned his Eagle Scout Rank, he invited John X to the Eagle Court of Honor where he surprised John by presenting him with an Eagle Mentor pin. An Eagle Scout may award this pin to an individual who has been an influence on the Eagle Scout's life. John was pleasantly surprised, and said he would cherish that pin forever. Anthony also surprised me by awarding me with an Eagle Mentor pin, in private, for my role in helping him with drumming throughout his life. Like John, it was truly an honor for me.

I only took a few lessons with John because at that time I was based in New York and had a commuter apartment in Queens where I stayed between flights/during layovers. I left California for New York the day before each trip, or series of trips, and if I had a series of two or three trips together, I would have one or two days off in New York in between each of them. That allowed me to spend some of my time off with other musicians I had met in New York, and go to jazz clubs to sit in on jam sessions where I was constantly learning from all these other top musicians.

I found that it was more convenient for me to study at Drummers Collective, a large school in Manhattan, and since I was there so much of the time, I could be more consistent with my lessons. They had practice rooms available for rent, so I was also able to practice whenever I was in town. Drummers Collective has since grown out of their original building and moved to a new, larger location, with a new name: The Collective School of Music. http://www.thecollective.edu

Kim Plainfield

http://kimplainfield.com

While at Drummers Collective, I studied with several world-class drummers, including Kim Plainfield. Kim is an Associate Professor at the Berklee School of Music, and is co-chairman of the faculty at Drummers Collective, where he has taught since 1979. His instructional book, *Advanced Concepts*, is known as the bible of modern progressive drumming. Kim has conducted countless clinics in Europe, the United States, Japan and Central America, as well as extended artist-in-residence programs at various conservatories in Europe.

At age 22, Kim was the drummer for the Pointer Sisters before he moved to New York. When I met Kim he was playing for Tania Maria, and when I was in town, if he was playing somewhere locally, he would invite me to come see the show.

One time, Kim was going to be in Paris performing with Tania Maria at the same time I was going to be in Paris for a 24-hour layover, and I went to see the show. During their intermission, Kim took me back stage to meet Ms. Maria, a lovely lady, who called me Cap-i-tan in her beautiful Brazilian accent.

A funny thing happened, well not so funny to the band members, during that show. Kim had been playing a long drum solo when the wooden backdrop fell forward, landing partially on him. The other musicians and stage hands finally got the backdrop upright and stabilized, while Kim, smiling all the time, kept on playing—like the Energizer Bunny! He received a tremendous, well deserved, round of applause from the appreciative Parisian audience when he finished his solo.

Tania Maria, however, wasn't the only musical star I met on that trip....

Max Roach

While I was sitting in the cockpit after finishing the pre-flight checks for a flight from New York to Paris, I happened to look back into the cabin to see how the boarding process was going. This was during the days before the cockpit door had to be closed while on the ground, so it was usually open. I saw a man sitting in the first row of Clipper Class who I recognized as Max Roach, the famous bebop era drummer who played with Clifford Brown, Charlie "Bird" Parker, Duke Ellington and countless others. I couldn't quite believe my eyes, so just to be sure, I asked the flight attendant to check the passenger roster. It really was Max Roach, so I sent a message to him that I was a drummer and a longtime fan of his, and would like to come back and chat with him during the flight. The flight attendants were of a younger generation and didn't know who Max Roach was, so I clued them in and asked them to treat him with special care. On my break I went back and we chatted for a while.

The drumming styles of today have all evolved from the earlier drummers. The top drummers of today will have studied all of the early drummers, including Max Roach, Art Blakey, Joe Jones, Philly Joe Jones, and many others. As an example: after studying the style of Art Blakey and Philly Joe Jones, one can hear the influence of those drummers in the playing style developed by the great Tony Williams. I was fortunate to have had about 20 lessons with Tony Williams in San Francisco, before his untimely death, when he was preparing to do an instructional drum video.

It turned out that Max Roach and I had a mutual friend, a famous drummer and sand dancer named Scoby Stroman, who knew every musician in New York and beyond. So we talked about Scoby and other musicians. Max was even interested in going to the club to see Kim Plainfield and Tania Maria that evening, but he had an early morning call for a drum clinic he was giving, and had to pass on going to the club.

About six months later, Mr. Roach was giving a concert at Kimball's East, a jazz club in the San Francisco Bay Area where we lived at that time, and Dee and I were able to attend. After the performance, we went backstage to say hello, and to my surprise he recognized me. He told his manager, who was standing next to him, that when he was on my flight we treated him like royalty. That was good to hear, because in the past black musicians of Mr. Roach's generation were treated like anything but royalty. In fact, the treatment was often very poor due to the double standards of the times, which meant they could play in white clubs, but could not stay in white hotels, and so on. Therefore, his statement really made me feel proud that my flight attendants had treated him so well. Before Max passed away in 2007, my wife and I were fortunate to be able to attend several of his concerts.

Scoby Stroman

Scoby Stroman was a wonderful man, and everyone who knew him loved him. I met him when he was in San Jose, California, performing with a friend of his, and we became instant friends. He lived in Brooklyn, and invited me to the jazz club where he ran a nightly jam session, so I could sit in and learn. This was a small club in the Bedford-Stuyvesant neighborhood—often referred to as Bed-Stuy—a predominately black area in Brooklyn. It was also a high crime area, although I didn't know that at the time. The first time I went to the club was before I had a car in New York, so I took the subway. It was summer and still daylight when I arrived at the club, but when I decided to leave, around midnight, Scoby insisted it was not safe for me to take the subway out of the neighborhood that late at night, and wouldn't let me leave until he got off work so he could drive me to my apartment in Queens.

    A lot of famous musicians who lived in New York would frequent the club when they were in town between tours, and there was a lot of good jazz to be heard there. Getting to sit in with some of those highly-talented musicians, such as saxophonist Branford Marsalis, bassist Andy McCloud, and pianist Rodney Kendrick, and having them be considerate of my not being anywhere near their level was an honor. Rodney and I became friends; we would hang out together in Manhattan and jam in a rented room at the Drummers Collective when time allowed. Andy McCloud, who recently passed away, also became a friend, and visited our home in California when he was there on tour with Jon Hendricks and Annie Ross.

During the last eight years of my flying career, our kids were all grown, so it was easier for Dee to accompany me to New York. We would meet up with Scoby and his fiancée to go out to dinner, or Scoby would take us to see a performance by some of his famous musician friends, such as pianist Randy Weston, and saxophonist Joe Henderson. It was truly a remarkable experience.

Being Hispanic, my wife has light brown skin. Most all of the musicians in the jazz club where Scoby ran the jam sessions were black. One evening, Dee and I were sitting at a table with Scoby and his fiancée when it was my turn to go sit in and play. When I sat down behind the drums, all of a sudden my wife yelled out, "Honey, you look like a ghost sitting up there," and the whole place roared with laughter.

In 1996, after I had retired and couldn't frequent New York any longer, I learned that Scoby passed away from complications following a stroke. He was an icon in New York, and everybody who was anybody in the New York jazz music scene attended his memorial service. He was a true friend and he is missed.

Mike Clark

http://www.mikeclarkmusic.com

Mike Clark was another of my instructors at Drummers Collective. Mike, like Kim Plainfield, is from the San Francisco Bay Area. Mike is an innovative funk-jazz drummer with a style that is difficult to emulate, and he's constantly in demand at drum clinics around the country. His book, *Funk Drumming: Innovative Grooves & Advanced Concepts*, was published by Hal Leonard and has become a bestseller.

Mike and I became good friends, and when he was in the Bay Area, we would get together to hang out for a while. He would come over to my house and tune my jazz drum kit for me and show me some new drum licks, or we would go to Jazz at Pearls, a club in San Francisco, to see some of the top local jazz musicians, such as our friends bassist John Witala, virtuoso guitarist Bruce Forman, and legendary drummer Vince Latiano. Vince played for the famous Cal Tjader Latin Jazz group during Cal's final years, 1979 to 1982, when Cal died of a heart attack.

Mike is a classic Type A personality, who is always in high gear. Since I'm a Type B personality it was hard for me to keep up with him—but it was great fun trying.

In 1973, Mike replaced drummer Harvey Mason and became the only white guy in Herbie Hancock and the Head Hunters group for the recording of "Thrust" in 1974. Mike is an interesting storyteller, with plenty of stories to tell about the Head Hunters' days. It seems he was constantly at odds with one of the other musicians, and one day it all came to a head; apparently there was actually a physical fight (or close enough), which effectively blew off the steam, and from then on the conflict stopped and they agreed to get along. I haven't seen Mike in a long time, but I recently found him on Facebook. Maybe one day his tours will take him through Phoenix, and we'll get to catch up. On the other hand, maybe Dee and I will go to New York again to see Mike and Kim—two superb musicians and wonderful individuals.

Preparing for Retirement: The Next Goal

In the '80s and '90s, with the age 60 rule still requiring that all airline pilots retire when they turn 60 years of age, regardless of ability, I was working on my next goal of becoming a professional musician once I was forced to quit flying. Then, after I retired from the airline I would practice as much as eight hours a day. I also played jobs with any band that would hire me, which was difficult because there were so many excellent drummers, far superior to me, who had been playing all their lives. However, I was determined, and managed to play with several good bands in the Bay Area fairly steadily.

I should say that despite all my lessons and practice, I knew I did not have the talent to be a great musician. Being a truly great musician requires a born talent, in my opinion, in addition to years of training and experience. One can train and practice, practice, practice, and become a good musician (and I did), and may be able to make a living in the music business; but to become a top musician takes talent. I didn't need to be the next Max Roach or Tony Williams; I just wanted to spend the next stage of my life doing something that I loved. I wanted to play music.

The Big Band: The Bill Travis Swing Orchestra

One day, after I had retired from flying, and my wife and I had adjusted to our new routines, I decided to call a band leader named Russ Button, a trumpet player who had a 17-piece band, to see if he could use a substitute drummer. Many times, the way to get a gig is to volunteer to sub at rehearsals. There are often times when a band's regular drummer can't make a rehearsal, so each band leader has a list of subs. Russ invited me to come sit in at a rehearsal the following week.

Because I wanted to have my own band that I could manage in my own way, and do my own bookings, after attending two rehearsals I offered to buy the band from Russ—and he agreed to sell it to me. When you buy a band, you buy the book of music, sound system, any equipment that may come with the band, and usually, the band name. Russ elected to keep his band name, so I purchased everything but the name, and decided to rename it the "Bill Travis Swing Orchestra." After selling the band to me, Russ continued to play in the band, and I was glad to keep his talents in the lineup for as long as I could.

A 17-piece band is a business, and has to be operated like one. The owner has to spend time marketing and promoting the band to the target audience. In addition to marketing, there is the job of keeping talented musicians interested in rehearsing because if the band doesn't rehearse, then it will not sound good on a gig.

The music we played was big band swing music from the '40s and '50s, such as Glenn Miller, Duke Ellington, Count Basie, and others of that era. Swing music is wonderful dance music, however, it's not individually challenging for a good musician. This style of music does need rehearsal to get the whole band playing tight together; that's what makes for a good sound. But what makes good musicians want to rehearse is to have challenging jazz charts to play. By challenging, I mean charts that are difficult to read and difficult to play, so that the musicians have a hill to climb and can increase their skills. It's very satisfying to work on a difficult chart for several weeks, finally getting the band sounding great, and then playing that chart at a jazz concert.

When I began booking the big band, I found that I didn't have as much time to practice as before. The booking and the job of searching for new and challenging music to buy for rehearsals took a lot of time. As a consequence, my playing sort of hit a plateau. Then there was the marketing, meeting with potential clients, scheduling the gigs, and scheduling the musicians for the gigs. There's also the job of making sure the sound system—amplifiers, speakers, microphones, and all the other paraphernalia such as music folders, music stands, etc., are all in place. So, I had to make a compromise between my roles as drummer and band leader.

Talented musicians are artists. They're good at what they do, but getting to the gig on time, and getting back on stage on time after breaks is something that some are not very good at. They need someone to push and make sure they're where they're supposed to be when they're supposed to be there.

This was in the '90s, and GPS was not prevalent at the time. Consequently, for every job, in order to be certain the musicians knew where the venue was, I would have to print a map, highlight the route, and write step-by-step directions to email to the musicians. We didn't have smartphones either, so it wasn't unusual for a band member to show up late, saying they couldn't locate the venue—which, when roughly translated, meant they left home late.

It took a few years to get the band rolling along smoothly. But finally, we had a high-quality sound system, attractive music stands, talented musicians, we were getting gigs, and the band sounded great. The full 17-piece big band only worked about twelve gigs a year; therefore, in order to support the band expenses and have gigs that paid more money per musician, I needed to have several smaller bands.

With the smaller bands, we could play a trio gig, or play gigs with either our 5-piece band, or the 7-piece band; we were very flexible. Because of the smaller bands, the musicians were able to play many more gigs and make more money. It's a struggle for a musician to make a living just playing music, so most of them had day jobs; they played music for the joy of music and a little extra money, like I did back when I was working in the Detroit factories.

Dee also got involved in the band business with me, and was a tremendous help. In fact, it would have been almost impossible for me to do it without her. Dee was the band coordinator, but referred to herself as the "Band Mom," and she was a strict mom. On a gig, whenever it was getting close to time to play, she would get all the musicians rounded up and on stage—on time. She knew every one of them, and had a good rapport with each.

As the band coordinator, Dee was the liaison between the event coordinator, or the bride when we played weddings, and the band. Since I was sitting behind the drums during the performances, it was extremely difficult for me to talk to the coordinator if they had to make a change in the evening's agenda; but Dee was able to work things out, and then communicate that to me, so I could plan the time and music in order to meet the changes.

We performed for a lot of weddings, and Dee was excellent at dealing with the brides, who would always appreciate her efforts to make their special day just that little bit more special. We had three daughters of our own, all married, so Dee knew how to work with brides. On the wedding day, the bride is under a tremendous amount of stress, and not everyone does so well under that kind of pressure. Dee would keep close watch, and if she sensed the bride was having difficulty and in need of assistance, she'd be straight over. She also carried a sewing kit, which was needed often, and a lot of tissues. It was always a pleasure to see Dee in action because she could keep everything under control—and keep the bride happy. That allowed me to concentrate on the music.

When the gig is over, musicians all want to leave quickly, sometimes not even bothering to put their music away; they would just leave it on the stand and walk out to their car. Well, Dee, the strict Band Mom, would not allow any of that. She would stand by the music cases with the pay checks, and in order to get their check they would have to deposit their music folder in the case, and fold up their music stand and chair. That would save me an hour's work after each gig; I was busy enough tearing down the sound system and loading everything into the van. The band did well, but we didn't earn enough to hire a roadie. That job was mine too.

Photo by Dee Travis

My years with the Bill Travis Swing Orchestra were very enjoyable, and I'm glad I was able to achieve my goal of working as a professional musician with my own big band. All of the hard work of managing the big band was absolutely worth the time and effort. The only thing better than sitting in front of and listening to the beautiful and powerful sounds of a 17-piece band is the excitement and joy of being in that band, helping to produce those magnificent sounds.

After a while, Dee and I decided to relocate to Phoenix, Arizona. Primarily, it was because the Bay Area was getting too expensive to live during retirement, and I didn't like the earthquakes. One of our daughters was already living in the Phoenix area, so we knew we could still visit California often, to visit our daughter there. That made it easier to make the move.

Manny Constancio

Having decided to relocate, I sold the Bill Travis Swing Orchestra, including the name, to my Musical Director, Manny Constancio. He is still operating the band under the same name, "The Bill Travis Swing Orchestra," and has the same website: www.btso.com.

Manny was the Commanding Officer of the United States Navy Band in San Diego until his retirement, when he returned to live and work in the San Francisco Bay Area. He is a brilliant musician who makes his living with music; therefore, I was more than happy that not only was the band continuing to operate without me, so the musicians could continue playing in the big band, but that it was doing so under Manny's capable leadership. Leaving California, with the big band now in the hands of Manny Constancio, I ended my career as a professional musician.

But life was not over—as you'll see in the following Epilogue….

Epilogue

My flying career was abruptly cut short in 1992 when I had BPPV and couldn't pass my FAA flight physical. My music career ended in 2004 when we moved to Arizona. It was only after we got settled in Arizona that I realized it would be too difficult to start building a band in a new city without already having contacts established. It would have taken three years to develop the necessary contacts, find good, reliable, professional musicians, and start getting gigs. Consequently, I decided to end the music career.

But I was far from being ready to retire and go fishing. I don't even like to fish. I don't have the patience or the skills, and no desire to go down that road. However, I did know that there were new and exciting roads to travel, and soon I started traveling down one of those roads to embark on a new career—real estate.

New Goals

I didn't mention it earlier in this book, but during the 1970s I had studied real estate, and was rehabbing homes during my days off from the Pan Am flights. After relocating to Arizona in 2004 and ending the music career, I still felt the need to keep busy doing something I love to do. After giving it a lot of thought, I decided to go back into real estate full time; so I set new goals of becoming a successful rehabber of homes, and to own my own real estate business.

With a lot of hard work, I achieved those goals.

During the past few years, I rehabbed about 20 homes. Today, I own my own real estate business, Captain Bill Realty, LLC, where I help residential home buyers and sellers in the Phoenix area. www.CaptainBillRealty.com

At the same time, now that I've begun to write, I've had the pleasure of reliving some of the highlights of my flying and music careers and sharing them with people who can relate to them; and especially, sharing them with people who might benefit from knowing that they can use visualization and goal setting techniques to realize their own dreams.

What's more, I've definitely caught the "writing bug," and I'm working on ideas for several books, including another inspirational book or two, and a follow up to *Pan Am Captain, Aiming High*, with more tales from the cockpit and exotic layovers.

Acknowledgements

Thanks to my lovely wife Dee, because without her support my Pan Am career would not have been possible. She sacrificed her own career, and didn't complain when I had to spend money we didn't have for expensive aviation education, knowing that it was for a good purpose.

When I got my first airline job, Dee became a stay-at-home mom to take care of the children and run the household, so that I could be the breadwinner. We were a team, and each had our individual responsibilities. The job Dee took on was tough, especially with four children and a husband who was out of the country almost half the time. In those days there were no cell phones for texting and easy daily communication; long-distance calls were expensive, and international calls were prohibitively expensive. It takes a very strong woman to stay in a marriage and raise a family under those circumstances. Dee is a very strong woman.

Our children, Art, Sandy, Connie, and Katrina, were very supportive and understanding, and under Dee's guidance they have all turned out to be outstanding citizens who now have their own families. They had to accept the fact that I could not be there to share in all of their moments. I was almost never home on Christmas Day, but we would have Christmas early, so we could celebrate it together as a family. While I missed many of their important milestones, my heart was with them, and I always made sure I could be there for the most important events, such as graduations and marriages.

Thanks to my daughter Connie, who, along with my wife and friends, convinced me to write this book. As a *reward*, Connie got to edit it for me, and Marissa did the final grammar editing. Dee performed the final content editing. Thanks to Dee, Katrina, Danielle, Connie, John, Madison, Marissa, and Anthony for their assistance in choosing the cover design.

My parents are no longer with us, but they deserve a very special thank you. It was with their understanding and support that I found the freedom to reach out and try to better myself. They were never critical of my decisions, even when those decisions may not have been the best. They were great, supportive parents, who allowed me to be myself.

Bill and Dee Travis

A Fit Sexy Body at Age 80

In the past, I would begin a physical fitness program, only to drop it after a period of time. When I embarked on those programs, the goal was to "keep in shape," which is only a statement; it isn't really a goal.

I didn't know what weight I wanted to carry, I didn't know what amount of body fat I needed to have, and I didn't know what I wanted my body to look like. That was a mistake. It was destined to fail because it was too easy to drop off the program.

Now I know that in order to be successful in a physical fitness program. I need to set—and visualize—short term, medium term, and long term goals.

My cardiologist told me for two years to lose 20 pounds; I said okay, but kept procrastinating. After getting numerous, good natured complaints from my wife about my protruding belly, having to buy larger sized clothes, and taking a close look at my body in the mirror, I finally had a reality check.

I realized that I didn't have the energy I once had, my six-pack abs had turned to six layers of saturated fat, and I didn't like the way my pear-shaped body looked.

I needed to listen to my doctor and my wife—I needed to make a change.

Consequently, on January 24, 2013, I started another fitness program—only this time there was a difference. I began training with a wonderful cross-fit trainer, Jeannie Glover, for the first few months through the beginner stage.

After several months, I modified my goals by deciding to build my body so that I could enter a bodybuilder Physique contest in July 2014, at the age of 80. The Physique competitor needs a "beach" type body that is symmetrical and muscular, but not the bulging type muscles of a bodybuilder.

After making that decision, I hired a professional bodybuilder and personal trainer, Robert Farrow, who has over 20 years' experience in both competition and training competitors. This is an ambitious project, but I have to aim high, and with Rob's guidance and my hard work, I will be on the stage competing in July 2014.

My new book will show how I was able to transform my body at age 80. It will provide guidance on nutrition, weight lifting exercises, cardiovascular exercises, and it will dispel some of the myths surrounding the subject of exercise and diet. It should be ready for publication around July 2014.

Here are some subjects to expect in the book:
- What Your Doctor Doesn't Tell You About Weight Loss
- How You Can Lose Body Fat and Gain Muscle at the Same Time
- What It REALLY Takes to Get Those 6-Pack Abs
- Are Your Hormones in Balance?
- Exercises You Can Do at Home
- Why You Should Hire a Personal Trainer
- The Dangers of Being Overweight or Obese
- What an Exercise Program Can Do For You

You can keep track of the book's progress and read excerpts as they become available on my website, www.PanAmCaptain.com

Feel free to send suggestions for material you would like to see included in the book. Email to: Book@PanAmCaptain.com

www.ingramcontent.com/pod-product-compliance
Lightning Source LLC
Chambersburg PA
CBHW050627300426
44112CB00012B/1691